1

Published by Phoenix Publishing
Registered Charity 1150955
Company No: 8317917
55 Cambridge Road
East Cowes
Isle of Wight, PO326AH

Printed in the United States of America

ISBN-10: 1977902502

Photography by
Mark Gilchrist, Brian Ryan, and David Crossman

Cover design: CiA

Get MAD!
The Life and Times of a Madwoman
by
Victoria Dunford

Phoenix Publishing
Isle of Wight, U.K.

With love, I dedicate this book to:

My mother, Larisa Scutaru

A strong and gentle soul who taught me to trust, believe in hard work and that so much can be done with little. I owe you a unique distinction, I owe you my life-literally and figuratively.

My brother, Oleg Scutaru,

for my education, my trip to the U.K., and everything you sacrificed in order that I might have.

My husband, John Dunford,

For your patience, love, friendship, humor, unfailing support, and the freedom you give me.

INTRODUCTION TO A MADWOMAN

Every now and then I've been lucky enough to meet some remarkable people: people who make a difference to the lives of others, with minimum resources and fuss. Victoria Dunford, BEM (a designation of recipients of the British Empire Medal, Britain's highest award to non-natives) is one such person.

I first encountered Victoria in late 2013 when she cajoled me into attending a presentation of 200 wheelchairs to Moldova's second city, Bălţi (pronounced Balts). Even more impressively, she had managed to simultaneously do the same to the Moldovan Minister of Social Protection, the Deputy Minister of Health, and the Mayor of Bălţi. I should have realised then that this was a sign of things to come!

Over the next three years I was to witness Victoria launch her campaign against some of the social injustices that exist in Moldova. First, she set about recycling unwanted NHS medical equipment: surplus to requirements in Britain, but life-saving in under-funded Moldovan hospitals. By giving them a new lease of life in Moldova, wheelchairs, hospital beds, specialist chairs from the UK, are helping patients 1,800 miles away.

That would have been more than enough for most small charities to handle. But Victoria had her sights on an even greater cause. In the space of just four months in 2015 Victoria managed to turn a derelict kindergarten building from the Soviet era into a comfortable, welcoming and spacious day care centre offering first class therapies and, well, life to children and teenagers with disabilities: Children who, hitherto, had been hidden away from society. Existing, but not living. Thanks to Victoria, her husband John and the commitment of numerous individuals and organisations (the Communication and Workers Union Humanitarian Aid deserve a special mention for their generosity), the Phoenix

6

Centre opened in September 2015 in Rîşcani, Moldova.

Resourceful as ever, Victoria even managed to persuade the Moldovan Prime Minister to inaugurate it! The behavioural change it has triggered since then in those attending the centre is nothing short of miraculous. For the first time, these children are now able to learn, develop and lead socially fulfilling lives just like any other able-bodied child.

On the face of it this book is the story of one woman's struggle and, ultimately, success in transforming the lives of some of the most vulnerable members of Moldovan society. But in so doing it shines a critical light on social inequality, staggeringly out-dated views on disability, mind-numbing bureaucracy and widespread avarice and corruption. A more sanguine assessment is that Victoria has turned on its head the notion that individuals cannot deliver positive change against the weight of the authorities and social stigmas. The Phoenix Centre has provided children who have been hidden away for years with learning and physical disabilities— Moldova's forgotten children—with a purpose to their lives for the first time.

Victoria describes herself as a little bit mad to have taken all this on. Mad or not, the Phoenix Centre is now a beacon of excellence and hope in the north of Moldova and is a testament to Victoria's tenacity, humanity and compassion. I urge you to read her story.

Phil Batson
British Ambassador to the Republic of Moldova, 2013-16
September 2017

A FORCE OF NATURE

I had the pleasure of meeting Victoria and John in 2014. In Victoria, it soon became evident that I was dealing with a force of nature. Here is someone, I thought, who embodies all that's best in humanity. Frankly, I am blessed with many in my circle of friends and acquaintances who answer that description. What most of them don't have, however, that Victoria does have - and in abundance - is the will to breath life into her vision, and the determination to subdue whatever obstacles might stand between her and its fulfillment. In such a confrontation, I could see, the obstacle has no chance.

The axiom 'behind every great man is a good woman,' is no less true in the reverse. Behind Victoria, every step of the way, is John. Though he eschews the spotlight - in fact runs from it - John is, in many ways, the motive force behind Victoria's vision. It is he whose compassion drew the needs of the disabled and elderly in Moldova to Victoria's attention, and who, operating in the background, works tirelessly to wrap sinew around the bones of her dreams.

Together, Victoria and John each possess qualities that make the other unconquerable and, in those rare instances when they need reminding what it's all for, they only need a glance into the eyes of a disabled child, and the vision, like the phoenix, is startled to life from the ashes of discouragement, frustration, and exhaustion, to rise again, and again, and again.

David Crossman - Bestselling author of *A Terrible Mercy*

FOREWORD

I opened the door to our neighbour Victoria one Summer evening in 2012.

'Hello, how are you? How do I start a charity?' she asked. Not being one for small talk, I've always appreciated Victoria's directness, but her question still took me by surprise. Little did I know what was about to unfold.

That evening, I had my first glimpse of Victoria on a mission. Working in our local NHS hospital, she had noticed the regular replacement of beds and medical equipment. Curious, she asked what happened to the 'old' items, and was shocked to hear that they went either into landfill or into expensive storage. She determined to find a way of sending some of the unwanted equipment to impoverished, badly equipped hospitals in her native Moldova, the poorest country in Europe. And for that, she needed to start a charity.

I had worked in and later with the UK voluntary sector since 1987 and as a leadership coach, I had for a time been on the UK National Council for Voluntary Organisations' (NCVO) list of approved consultants. I had no idea how to start a charity, but I still had one of NCVO's charity directories on my bookshelf and I passed it over with as much encouragement as I could muster unprepared. Our other neighbour, John Barnes, had a lot of experience of running local charities, and Victoria sought his advice too.

Within weeks, John, my husband Peter, Ruslan Ciobanu, a Moldovan manager at a local farm, and I were trustees of a brand new registered charity, MAD-Aid (Make a Difference). We were soon joined by Sean Colson, a local business owner whose company also had a base in Moldova. From the beginning, Victoria's husband John did everything he could to make things happen, and has been Victoria's rock ever since. Later, when Ruslan resigned, we were joined by businessman Iurie Bivol.

9

The charity launched in September 2012, and Victoria secured attendance at the launch event from the Moldovan Embassy in London, the local Moldovan community and our local MP. Two friends and I agreed to provide entertainment at a fundraising event in November, another piece of MADness for which I am deeply grateful, since we still sing together five years later.

The first year was entirely hand-to- mouth. Victoria worked full time, running the charity in her spare time. The challenges were endless. She obtained a waste management license that allowed us to collect and dispose of the equipment. She set up a sister charity to manage the Moldovan end of the transport and to handle the gargantuan task of inventorying and distributing the equipment. None of what we sent would end up being siphoned off and sold. She and her husband John persuaded local businesses to help with donations and free storage. Local Rotary Clubs lent their weight. We all rolled our sleeves up at one time or another, when we were needed, but the major heavy work was done by Victoria and John, together with family members and local Moldovan-born friends who understood just what a difference this work could make.

For a while, we (the Trustees) expected that we would be raising funds to send up to three trucks a year to Moldova, an annual total of about £10 - 12,000.

We had no idea. Fundraising was still very patchy when Victoria first unveiled her plans to open a day centre for disabled children, and a healthcare facility for adults at a disused spa and health centre in Mihaeleni, her home village. To say that we were nervous would be an understatement. The Salvia Centre was enormous, dilapidated, a huge undertaking. I think we were quietly relieved when Victoria discovered that Salvia was no longer owned by the village and could not be developed in the way she wanted. She must have been tired of our constantly trying to slow her down, as we felt we must at that stage.

As the hospital equipment transfer settled down, Victoria turned her attention to wheelchairs. On a recent visit to Moldova, she had met mobility-impaired children who had no means to leave home to go to school or have any sort of social life. Daily existence for them and their families was very hard. Before long, with the support of Island Mobility and our local prison service, we were sending truckloads of reconditioned wheelchairs to Moldovans who needed them.

Meanwhile, Victoria had not given up on the idea of opening a day centre for disabled children and young people, and an early intervention facility for babies with disabilities and their parents. She was offered a 49-year, rent-free lease on a former kindergarten on the edge of Rîşcani, in the north of Moldova.

It was this project above all that cemented my admiration for Victoria's no-nonsense determination. She developed a cast-iron ability to show people her vision and get them behind her. She questioned herself constantly, but when she secured the support of Communication Workers' Union Humanitarian Aid (CWUHA) to refurbish a part of the building, we knew that it would happen and that we must support it. Victoria drove the work, cajoling, pushing, demanding high quality and getting it, determined to open in time for CWUHA's 2015 autumn aid convoy. And she did, competing not just the refurbishment project but the recruitment of specialist staff to work with the children and run the centre.

John Barnes and his wife Ann attended the opening in September 2015, just three years after the charity started. It was to be John's only visit. Sadly, he died in January 2017, still thinking about and working for us in his hospital bed.

We miss him hugely. Peter, Ann and I visited Phoenix in May 2017 and were moved and impressed to meet the children and to see their progress, and to understand the

11

huge difference made by our dedicated and skilled team of therapists and teachers.

How had all this happened in less than five years? Quite simply because of Victoria's vision, energy, determination and willingness to learn, that have gained the trust and support of our partners and the committed help of many volunteers. I had no idea what was coming when I opened the door that summer evening, but I'm truly grateful to have played a small part in getting MAD-Aid off the ground.

Victoria's book is both an inspiration, and a call to action. I hope you will enjoy reading it as much as I have.

Ann Lewis
Chair
MAD-Aid
September, 2017

Index

Get MAD!
The Life and Times of a Madwoman
by Victoria Dunford

Part One

'Impossible!' is Just the Beginning

Chapter One

You Can't Get There From Here

'Where is Moldova?'

This is a standard question I am asked when I tell people where I'm from. Moldova is a small country that many choose to ignore, not knowing where it is situated. But I'm lucky to call this small piece of landlocked territory my homeland. Yes, it's the poorest country in Europe, but for me it was perfect, it was special. The white winter nights and hot summers bring so many memories to my mind.

Traditions were at the core of our identity. In the summer in the villages, most people worked in the fields. The children took the cows and sheep out to graze in the morning and brought them back in the evening. The work days during this busy time of year were 14-16 hours long, and the work was accompanied by laughter and smiles and the enjoyment of life.

Sundays and Orthodox holidays were like a hymn for the country, especially in rural areas. No one worked on those days. That was the way people recharged and kept going. All the gardens were full of fruit and vegetables starting with strawberries and cherries, and ending up in autumn with apples and grapes. And then, on the short winter days, people worked only 5-6 hours, mainly to clear the snow and feed the animals. In the evening the neighbors would get together and play cards, tell jokes and life stories. Children would be laughing, sledging, and playing in the snow.

This is how I remember it.

To many in the west, this may seem a primitive way of life—more existing than living—but there's truth to the saying 'ignorance is bliss.' Folks didn't know what they were missing, so they were happy with what they had. The camaraderie that evolved from shared struggle—the warmth, friendship, and mutual support, formed the core of everyday life.

Then there was me.

I was different. I'd always been described that way. Someone would tell me, 'You want too much from life. Be content with what you have,' and, more than once, I heard, 'You're a woman. Leave men's work to the men.'

Why wasn't I content with the way things were? Why didn't I just slip into the groove, like a needle on a record player, and join in the song that everyone else was singing— the song they'd always sung?

I don't know. I can't point to any single event that made me question the way things were, or why I thought things should be, or could be better. It was just a feeling, a feeling that, in time, became an irresistible conviction. And it's following that conviction that—for better or worse—has made me what I am today, either 'inspirational', or 'mad', depending on whom you ask.

I lived in a small village, Mihaileni, in northern Moldova, and even as a schoolgirl, I always looked for new opportunities, took every intelligence test, every IQ competition, and tried to be one of the best pupils in school. I got along with everyone, though I found playing and talking about boys boring. I loved reading books, talking to elderly people and learning about their life experiences. I was restless to grow up. Silly, I know.

My father died while my mother was pregnant with me. Many people in the village thought that, because of all the stress, I would be born with mental disabilities. Many medical workers, as well as some friends and relatives, advised my mother to terminate her pregnancy. She was only 30 years old and already had my 6-year-old brother to care for.

This illustrates a predominant trait of Moldovans: they're intrusive. They always know what's best and—with good intentions of course—are always ready to offer their advice. Mom listened politely to everyone but—much to their chagrin—decided not to kill me by having an abortion.

So I was born, a copy of my father.

Mother dedicated her life to my brother, Oleg, and me, and worked to give us every advantage she could. Oleg only went to college periodically in 90s because regular attendance was beyond our means. When my time came, and I finished school, he promised himself that he would support me to have the education I wanted, and he did his best to keep that promise; He left Moldova and worked mainly in Russia just to help me get a university education.

I went to State University in Chisinău, the capital of Moldova, and discovered a new, different world—a very busy one! After my first year at University I decided that I would learn more, faster, if I arranged private lessons for myself. I wanted to have private English lessons, computer lessons, and driving lessons—all impossibly out of reach as I was on an extremely tight budget. Also at that time it was very rare for women to have a driver's license. So during my last year at school when we were offered driving courses, my mother said I couldn't have a license until my brother had his, as he was boy and older. (Truth be told, he still doesn't have one!)

Five years later, as a graduation present, he paid for me to get one.

In my fourth year at university, high-achieving students were given the opportunity to apply to work during the summer holiday in the United Kingdom. I jumped at the chance, was selected, and got a visa.

I was ready to discover a new world, a new adventure. So it was that, in 2004, for the first time in my life, I left Moldova.

I arrived in Gatwick airport with four boys from different Moldovan universities. We were assigned to a farm in Canterbury for six weeks and for another eight weeks to a farm in Lewes, near Brighton.

Getting out of Gatwick and being taken by bus to

With my big brother Oleg

Canterbury was like living in a movie. Everything seemed so unreal, so perfect. I'd read many books about English queens and kings and tea time, but never thought as I read them that

I would ever actually see Hyde Park or Buckingham Palace.

Upon arrival in Canterbury, we were shown the caravan in which we would live for next few weeks. We used to walk a few miles to shop and always marveled that nearly every household we passed on the way had one or two cars. That explained why so few people were walking.

In Moldova only a few families out of the whole village had a car, and that would be a Russian make such as Lada or Moscvici. Today there are many foreign cars—especially in the cities—but in 2004 it was still rare.

While the universities in Moldova gave only top students this opportunity to work abroad, in the U.K. our education only qualified us to pick strawberries, which had nothing to do with our degrees. I decided the system must be a winnowing process, to discover those most likely to work hard in order to get ahead.

After the first placement, we were sent to a place called Culver farm, harvesting sweetcorn. Every Saturday, our day off, we used to go sightseeing in Brighton, and it was there I had yet another experience: on our first visit to this nice seafront city, we witnessed a gay pride parade. We were absolutely stunned and amazed at this degree of freedom and at the way people cheered and respected this. In Moldova, all these years later, homosexuality is still considered a crime, and gay people are still not free.

England captured my heart, but with such mixed feelings. I was thinking of how lucky are the children born here, and how lucky are the families living here. Half of me wanted to go back home, half of me wanted to remain here. Ultimately, though, the decision wasn't too hard as I was due to complete my last year at University. I wasn't about to throw four years of hard work out the window, so when my contract was finished, I went home to Moldova.

Back at the university, preparing for my finals—having already started the work in Real Lyceum in Chisinău—I was

21

constantly trying to figure out how could I get back to U.K., learn all I could, and come back to Moldova and implement that type of farming and the business models there. At the back of my mind, though, was doubt: would it really be better for my people? Why not just let them continue with their backward practices and traditions and be and happy in their ignorance?

Until 1991, Moldova was part of Soviet Union, so, while traveling within the Soviet Union was easy, outside, it was pretty much impossible. When Moldova became independent, the analogy we always made was, the cage was open, but no one knew how to fly! Our minds were still locked in that small cage. The people were scared to discover new opportunities, scared to say yes to anything new or to any change.

I guess the answer to my question was that I felt it was time to let them know they had a choice. If they chose to live the way they had always lived, fine. But if they felt they had a potential that couldn't be realized by that life, they had a right to know their options.

Just a few months after graduation—and working for a while as a teacher—I put my diploma aside. Though I loved chemistry, my diploma was not appreciated and jobs for which I was qualified were poorly paid.

I left teaching and went to work stacking shelves at Metro, one of first shopping centres in Moldova. My wages at Metro were considerably better than they had been teaching; and I mean a huge difference. My teaching wages, as a new graduate, started at 600 lei per month, (about £25), while at Metro I earned 2600 lei, (£115).

Within six months of joining Metro I was promoted to Department Supervisor and was on track to move to a new store as Department Manager. Always, though, in the back of my mind was the dream of going back to the U.K., and I never gave up in my efforts to do so. So, after a long fight and a huge struggle with the Embassy and with my visa and expenses, I managed to get another contract for two years' work experience in England; this time on the Isle of Wight. I didn't care; for me all that mattered was that it was in the U.K..

In November 2006 I arrived at Ryde Esplanade, the ferry terminus on the Isle of Wight, and a taxi was waiting to take me to Wight Salads Farm. I sat in the driver's seat—I had forgotten it was right-hand drive! I arrived at the farm and started work the very next day. This time I knew I had two years to make the most of it, learn all that I could, including speaking English, which, despite my obsession with the U.K., I spoke only enough the get by. I also knew that I had to save every penny so that when I returned to Moldova I'd have capital to buy a flat and, hopefully, start a business.

These skills—added to my knowledge of exactly what I wanted in life—were a huge advantage. I was determined to focus on my dreams and allow very little time for anything that wouldn't help me achieve my goals. However, even knowing exactly what you're aiming at, and where you going, life can bring the unexpected. When I least expected, everything changed.

It was summer, 2007. A few of us decided to go to the beach for a barbecue. One of our British friends brought along his friend, John. He seemed quite interesting but very quiet as well. With my broken English I tried to have a conversation. By the end of the day we managed to joke to the extent that he threw me into the sea, and I couldn't swim! I managed to tell him just in time, and he got me out.

John felt guilty about this so he invited my friend and me to his house for dinner. He offered to show me the beautiful Isle of Wight where he was born and raised, and of which he is intensely proud. I had lived for nearly a year on the island by then, but I was not aware of its beauty and hidden amazing places. Somehow without expecting it, and definitely not according to my original plan, we started seeing each other.

We fell in love.

When I left Moldova I promised my mother that I'd return, and there was no way I would ever stay in the U.K.. I still think and feel that way occasionally. After we started seeing each other, all I could think of was that I wanted to show John Moldova, the way he had showed me his home. I wondered what he'd think when he saw it.

I got my chance in 2008 when we got married and went to Moldova for first time, as a sort of honeymoon.

John came with his brother. Their reaction was, well, the driving is bad, the roads are bad, but the people are amazing. They couldn't believe that my mother's house was so large, but the toilet was a hole in a shed in the yard—not a proper bathroom like they were used to. The water came from a well, drawn with buckets, a skill John learned very quickly. The neighbors would walk in and out of the yard and help each other, borrowing some sugar, or a garden tool, or helping to take the cow into the field. The garden was large and full of all types of vegetables, grapes and many fruit trees. Everything for John and his brother seemed strange, unreal, backward and amazing at the same time.

John's brother said he would return—a promise he has yet to keep—but John loves it and looks forward to each return.

Moldova is a beautiful country. And even though I tell people I live on the Isle of Wight these days, Moldova is where my heart is. It's something I can't explain, but it tugs at me like a magnet, even after all these years away.

I managed to convince John to take his yearly holidays—twice a year—in Moldova. You couldn't really call them holidays, because they weren't very restful or relaxing. But he knew that going to Moldova was important to me. In many ways it inspired me. While each return made me realize how different my new life was, I still called Moldova—and especially my mother's house—my home. In those early days, when I straddled those two worlds, John was both my anchor and the string on my balloon. Through all that was to come, he was my rock, always encouraging me and giving me the strength to carry on when I had no strength left.

The transition has been far from smooth or easy. Living two lives is difficult. Being called an immigrant used to hurt. I was often criticized or made fun of for my accent, or when my grammar was incorrect when writing. But in order to get ahead, and to grow as a human being, I had to ignore those things or, in the words of a popular song *Shake It Off!* To constantly remind myself that it's all part of a wonderful experience. And, most importantly, that if I focus on my goals and work hard to achieve them rather than the little negative things, I can do it.

But I also discovered that those who are the most successful, and live the most worthwhile lives, are those who retain their humanity, and demonstrate it through their care for others. I learned to accept myself, to recognize the mistakes I made along the way as part of life. In fact, to a great extent, they're how life teaches us lessons, and only by learning from those lessons do we grow. This understanding also helps me be gracious with other people's mistakes.

I was born in a village in Moldova, with muddy roads, no inside toilet, and intermittent electricity. But I got to where I am today because of Moldova. So, where am I today?

Chapter Two

The Shocking Reality

John loves early September in Moldova as the temperature is just right and the seasonal vegetables and fruits are, in his words, so much tastier than in England. So, in September 2009 we went to Moldova. But never could we have imagined how that trip would change our lives—and our attitude toward life—forever. Not only that, it would change many other people's lives. We had reached that place where, as the poet says, 'two roads diverge in a wood', and we took the road less traveled.

My mother was suffering badly with pain in her knees, so the three of us went to Bălți (pronounced Balts) to see an orthopedic doctor and, as we expected, she was scheduled for immediate surgery.

John visits Mum (Larisa Scutari) in hospital. Inspiration!

The hospitals in Moldova are set up in such a way that everyone brings their own bedding, blankets and pillows, cups and cutlery. If you don't you will end up with those that the hospital provides which are, respectively, stained, ripped, bent, and broken. So, I went home to get everything necessary for Mum—Larisa—to check in for her surgery that was scheduled for the next day. John looked puzzled. 'How can you bring stuff from home into a sterile environment?' he asked. 'Surely you don't need cups and plates!'

Well, the next day I took John with me to the hospital and he was shocked. So was I . . . at his reaction. I just couldn't understand his problem. He said, 'Victoria, this hospital's worse than those we had in World War Two.' He was saying this about the hospital I'd brought Mum to because it was the best in the region. Much better than the one in Rîşcani!

For ten days while my mother was in hospital, I spent 12-14 hours a day beside her, while John would pop in for 5 minutes at a time and stay in the car for rest of the day. He couldn't bear the poverty, the smell, the thought of the people having to go through that. I tried to understand him, and respected that he felt it unbearable to be in the hospital; however, it was still hard to comprehend why he was so strange about this. Up until now, he'd seen Moldova as a poor country with lovely people. In his words: 'Not Third World, just a Two-and-a-half World.'

John knew the country had its drawbacks—the roads were bad, the civic infrastructure unreliable—those things he could put up with, but not the conditions in the hospitals.

He was beside himself. When my mother was brought back from surgery, she was extremely disheveled and in great pain. I thought that we were losing her in front of our eyes. I knew she had a problem with blood pressure, so I asked the nurse to check it for her. This was not a simple procedure. There were holes in the manual blood pressure tube and, in the end, it took three of us to plug the holes and get the reading. All the while, of course, Mum continued in pain. She needed morphine, but there was none. I remember as if it were today, running up and down in the elevator in that hospital, with $300 in my pocket—a huge amount for Moldova—trying to find a doctor I could cajole, beg, or bribe to procure some strong medication.

Day after day, John would walk in, trying to be polite, say hello and get out. On one of these visits he noticed how the defibrillator had two wires sticking out where the pads should be. He noticed the smallest detail, and he really couldn't bear the smell, even if everything seemed to have been made to look as clean as possible. He would keep asking his rhetorical questions—Why was such and such not done properly? I'd listen to him, but was still baffled why he got so upset. To me, the cracked tiles, ripped linoleum, broken bedside cabinets, rusty metal beds, thin, stained mattresses, crowded rooms where IV drip bags hung from clothes hangers, were normal. To John, they were unspeakable horrors. And the list went on and on.

A few months later in spring 2010 I started working at St Mary's, our local hospital on the Isle of Wight. And then it was my turn to be shocked, as though hot and cold waves hit me at the same time. Suddenly and very quickly I understood John's thinking, I understood the way he looked at Moldova's healthcare system. It made me realize that it is impossible to set a time difference; 50 years probably were not enough. It was impossible to compare the two.

It was not just the conditions, but also the attitude, the approach to treatment and care. Everything was so unreal for me. I recalled the moment when I had to ask the nurse to check my mother's blood pressure after her major surgery, and in U.K. the nurses were doing it every 30 minutes to every patient who had any surgical intervention, even the smallest one.

The electric blood pressure meters, heart monitors, pain

infusion pump. The bedding was changed every day, a few times a day if needed! Every patient was treated equally. The only thing the hospital here was interested in was the patient's name, not their bank balance, nor how many relatives they had, or if anyone would be able to bring your bedding.

Clearly things needed to change at hospitals in Moldova. But how could I change them? Bălți hospital was one of the best! Elsewhere in Moldova things standards were much lower.

Things were about to get worse.

One day John and I visited the main children's hospital in Moldova, the Mother and Child hospital in Chisinău, the capital of Moldova. And here was yet another wake-up call. The beds were so rusty, the nurses explained that in the summer they have to take them out and wash with petrol to remove the rust.

In a room with six beds, there were, on average, two bedside lockers, and these had been repaired, poorly, many times. The bedsprings poked through the thin, dirty mattresses. And you could see pain in parent's eyes as they didn't have any choice but to put their children through this terrible experience.

The X-Ray machine had been in use since 1959. It was rusty and the images were still being developed in a darkroom. The surgery table and the extremely rusty beds left me speechless. In one way I thought, 'hold on, we can change this and that', and in other way I was feeling so useless and small in comparison with all these problems. You can only come to understand my words when you see both extremes—the U.K.'s perfect hospitals and the Moldovan ones.

I'd always wanted to become a doctor, however the circumstances (being born in Moldova and raised just by my mother and older brother) made that an unrealistic dream. So working in a hospital in the U.K., even as an assistant, was, in the beginning, extremely rewarding and enjoyable. At the same time, it made me despondent over conditions in Moldova.

Many times I would fantasize how wonderful it would be to show Moldovans a British hospital ward, to explain to Moldovan hospital workers that, you are here by choice, patients are not. All sorts of ideas crept into my head. As a quick learner, I soon knew my job inside and out and it soon became repetitive and boring. I needed to be challenged.

Again I thought about becoming a doctor. I contacted the University in U.K. and got all the paperwork in order to apply to become a doctor at this stage. After analyzing all the possibilities and challenges ahead, and my broken English skills, I soon understood that it was simply too late in life to take on the challenges of preparing myself for that profession. So I carried on working, slowly becoming extremely unhappy. Along the way I did a few more care assistant jobs in nursing homes in the community. I always got told that I was extremely good at it, but I wanted more, wanted to be able to use my brain. However in Moldova people were happy to have a job, any job.

Why had I wanted to become a doctor, I asked myself. In answer was that I wanted to help people; to change lives for the better. In fact, looking back over my life, I think that has always been my goal.

I mentioned this to John. He thought for a moment, then said: 'You don't have to be a doctor to do that.'

I considered this as I thought about the shocking reality of hospitals in Moldova. Life in the U.K. had also made me aware of the grinding poverty that is a daily reality in Moldova; the World Bank even labeled Moldova the poorest nation in Europe.

How could a nation with such rich soil and agricultural diversity be so poor?

I was born in there. My mother worked in various jobs when she needed to and, when times were really hard, went abroad to find work. We were not rich, but we had all the basics. I went to university. I knew few really poor families but in my childish mind I always felt they were to blame for their poverty; to some extent I do this now even more.

I saw families who couldn't send all their children to school every day as they didn't have clothes for all of them. I saw that in the 21st century there were still—however rarely—some families for whom electricity was an unaffordable luxury. That's when I began to understand that this was not the country I remembered, or maybe it was a reality I had been blind to, or simply chosen not to recognize.

Even worse, I came to realize that, though Moldova is blessed with rich land, and hard-working and ingenious people, endemic corruption and obstructionist government bureaucracy kill the very innovation and entrepreneurship the country needs to compete and thrive in the international marketplace.

Responsible leadership and adequate education could transform Moldova into a pleasant and prosperous country in which to live and raise a family. But until rising generations are educated to adopt consistent ethical and moral standards—including the abolition of bribery—and require their government officials to do the same, that potential will never be realized.

After I'd taken John to visit my school he'd said he couldn't understand how any of us could have learned anything with such archaic schooling. I explained that ours was the Soviet style of learning.

'But it's all rote,' he said, 'just feeding back to the instructor what he wants to hear. There's no place for logical thinking. No debate or discussion. How can you discover what's best if exploration's not an option? You can't have vigorous, or even meaningful, education without the kind of analysis that comes from open-minded thinking.'

I knew he was right, and, once again, I was overcome by the conviction that things have to change.

I understand, of course, that everyone is responsible for their own choices—and the consequences of those choices. But how can people make informed decisions when they're uninformed? When they're systematically kept in the dark about their about their rights, about the value of their thoughts and ideas, about their personal potential and their options—even about their significance as human beings?

Like an ancient tree that no longer bears fruit, the roots of division in Moldovan society go deep. They must be torn up. Positive forward motion demands co-equal collaboration of all the actors on the civic stage: national, regional, and local governments, academics, working people, churches, schools, government and non-government agencies, local and international organizations.

But even the adoption of revolutionary measures in all these fields is doomed to fail without popular resolve.

So, I'm dreamer. But without dreamers, how can dreams come true? Besides, I can prove that dreams come true. Not through magic, but through 'blood, sweat, and tears' and the willingness to subordinate short-term desires to long-term goals.

This perspective is just as important for you as an individual as it is for a nation; and it will enable you to focus your energies on that goal and make it a reality.

By now you're probably thinking: 'She's MAD!'

John would agree.

Chapter Three

'If you don't like it, change it!'

The difference between Moldovan and British hospitals and the approach to care unsettled me and daunted me daily. I could see that something needed to be done back home. Something drastic. But what, and how, and where, and by whom? The list of unanswered questions never ended.

Working in NHS, I started noticing room for improvement there, too. However, when I would make one of these mental observations, I was immediately reminded of conditions in Moldova and suddenly everything in the NHS wasn't so bad after all.

I never lost my Moldovan spirit and always tried to do what I believed to be right and correct. And I was always working. Many of my co-workers seemed to feel that I was trying to get above my station—after all, I was only an immigrant. But they were right! I was aiming to get above my station. And if there was anything I could learn, any skill I could acquire for free—lessons, courses, seminars, hands-on training—I'd be at the front of the line! I always said yes to extra shifts. If we were asked to volunteer, my hand was the first one in the air—often the only one. It wasn't easy. My co-workers were resentful because, quite honestly, I worked harder than they did.

One spring day, sitting with John in our front room after work, discussing events of the day, I mentioned that the NHS hospital where I worked was just about to replace lots of furniture and equipment. 'How great it would be if all those beds and other pieces could go to the cardiology ward in Rîșcani hospital,' I said dreamily. (That was where my mother was still a frequent patient).

John, who has always been a supportive husband, said: 'Well you can make it happen. Find out how, make a plan, and let's do it!' That slight push was all I needed. With his approval and confidence in me, I *could* make it happen! I don't know how many people have the blessing of a partner who will go the extra mile to help fulfill their dreams, but I know I couldn't have done it without him.

You have to act fast to get a photo of John!

I was determined not to let the grass grow under my feet. That same evening, I went to see my neighbor Ann, knowing that she has worked in the non-profit sector. Imagine you are having your tea or relaxing in the evening and there's a knock on your door with a bombshell question: 'How do I start a Charity?'

Once she was able to catch her breath, she reminded me politely that it was a long time ago that she was employed for a non-profit, and now she was in HR, but she'd give it a think and get back to me.

I settled myself for a long wait. Ann was a busy woman and I'd given her a lot to think about. So imagine my surprise when, not even an hour later, she showed up on my doorstep brandishing a book she still had from the National Council for Voluntary Organizations (NCVO), which listed hundreds of non-profit organizations, with a short description of each.

After I'd thanked her and she'd left, I began scanning every page, and couldn't wait to working hours to start calling and asking questions. At the same time, at the back of my mind, I couldn't silence an impression that charity work was for the idle rich, something to keep them busy when they were bored. I wondered if I was getting in over my head.

Nevertheless I carried on. I think it took me about five calls until, finally, someone directed me toward Community Action Isle of Wight, an organization of volunteers who put people on the right path to setting up a charity. I called them the next day and booked an appointment. Because my command of English was still poor, and I was very aware of my accent, my self-confidence was extremely low at the time, so I took John along. He rarely spoke, but his presence gave me the strength and confidence I needed.

Even now I go to every meeting/conference/seminar and it doesn't matter how much printed information is in front of me, I still take notes. At this particular meeting when every word was so new, I ended up with dozens of pages. I still have them. Estelle, my consultant/advisor, told me exactly the steps I needed to take to form a charity organization, and helped me understand the workings of the regulatory agency and governing board.

When I left, I had pages and pages of notes, so I felt I had a fair idea of the work that lay ahead.

I didn't have a clue.

Estelle told me that, first of all, I'd need a constitution. From my very Moldovan perspective, I thought, 'Countries have constitutions, why do I need one to send a truck of furniture to Moldova?' Then she said I would need a Board; well I thought, because of my broken English, she must think I was planning to build furniture. Why else would I need boards? But I kept listening patiently and taking notes. She also told me about a fundraising seminar that was coming up and offered us free spaces, so that we would have an opportunity to network, and to talk with and learn from other charities.

That afternoon, I went home and combed through my English notebook page by page. After hours of study, I understood all the puzzling words in Estelle's presentation. I made my checklist:

- Find the trustees
- Find a name
- Write the constitution
- Launch the charity
- Raise the aid
- Raise some money
- Make A Difference
- And endless other things.

At home or at work, all I could think about was getting started!

On top of all my U.K. work, I sought advice from friends and associates in Moldova, telling people I knew were in non-profits what I intended to do and how I aimed to do it. Being me—naive and honest—I expected everyone to say, 'Oh yes, this is very good. Just what Moldova needs!' Instead, all I heard was: 'Don't even think about it. You'll never get past the border. The bureaucracy will eat you alive! You'll never make money like this!' Well, making money was not my aim, however everyone's first question seemed to be: 'Why do you need this? What will you get out of it?'

36

What did I do? I listened to everyone politely, and ignored them.

I was confident at this time that we could easily overcome obstacles with simple logic. After all, I thought, border control officers are human, too. Surely they would respond positively to my attempt to bring aid to hospitals in Moldova.

I had a lot to learn.

In Moldova, everyone has a hand out. Bribery is taken for granted*. It's the way all public service workers—who are grossly underpaid—supplement their incomes.

I was determined to break that cycle. Every dollar, every pound, every piece of equipment or furniture I hoped to bring into the country was precious. It would change lives. Save lives! I thought, 'There must be a way! We need legislation!'

About this time I learned what would become another of my all-time favorite quotes: 'If you want it, you'll find a way. If you don't, you'll find an excuse.'

So, there was me: no experience, no expertise, no money, and very little time on my hands. All I had was a vision—more like a dream or a wish, really—and a stubborn determination to make it a reality. I had one other thing, though, a husband who ignored the height of the mountain set before us and just said, 'You don't have to jump to the top, Victoria. Just climb, one step at a time.'

At that time, we were expecting this to be a small charity: its only job being to get relief materials from NHS hospitals in the U.K., to hospitals in Moldova. How hard could that be? So, from that perspective, the mountain before us didn't really seem all that daunting. I felt that, if I could enlist the aid of Ann and two other neighbors as trustees, the work would be easily manageable. We all had jobs, families, and other obligations, of course, but I figured if each of us put in two or three hours a week, that would keep things running smoothly.

The very first Trustee meeting took place on 2nd of August 2012. John came up with the name: MAD-Aid, which stands for 'Medical Aid Delivered, Make a Difference'. The pros and cons of the acronym were debated endlessly, but John's idea won out, mainly because we couldn't come up with anything else that came as close to capturing our intent. It's even more appropriate now.

Soon after this meeting I went to Moldova to do some research. That's when I got my first glimpse at the size of that metaphorical mountain! And it was made of paper! The labyrinth of archaic and obstructionist laws and rules regulating the import of humanitarian aid was dizzying, and working my way through it was tedious and time-consuming, but not enough to scare me.

Government record keeping in general was poor; regarding the disabled, it was almost non-existent. I had to rely on UNICEF statistics, and the numbers were shocking. Worse yet, the reality of conditions in Moldovan hospitals— now that I was looking at them from my perspective after three years working in the NHS—were dismal. It had been only three years since John's visit in 2009, but now I was seeing things as he had: analytically and with a critical eye.

Where, aside from providing materiel to hospitals, could we do the most good?

I inquired about services for people with special needs—especially children, since that's where our hearts were. Once again I was astonished at how completely abandoned this population was. Ultimately, our resources forced us to make a choice between children with terminal disease and the disabled. After much soul-searching and debate, we settled on the latter because that's where we felt we could do the most.

I returned to U.K. with a heavy heart, having come to the realisation that the policy-makers in Moldova simply didn't care about those I was most desperate to help. They expressed no interest in my plans and proposals, and certainly no intention of joining me in the work. It was a slap in the face, I admit, but now I knew what I was dealing with and that's all that mattered; I would be getting no help from the government. I prepared to launch the charity.

The date was set for 1st of September 2012. We found a venue, spoke to other members of the Moldovan community on the Isle of Wight and divided the tasks. I invited the Moldovan Embassy from London and the Member of Parliament for the Isle of Wight.

Together with the Trustees, I prepared a presentation outlining our aims and our short and long-term objectives. Admittedly, because we had to put it together so quickly, it wasn't very slick or professional, but it laid out our intentions at that stage, which were that MAD-Aid would:

1. Help improve the conditions in Moldovan hospitals by transporting specialist furniture and equipment from the U.K. to Moldova
2. Convert the Salvia Centre, a disused public building in my home village that once served as a rehabilitation centre, and transform it into facility mainly for disabled children
3. To provide equipment (such as wheelchairs) to people with disabilities in order to bring them out of isolation.

The event was also our first fundraiser. We raised about £800 and we had a nice donation of £750 from a local company owner where one Moldovan was manager. For our small charity, this was very encouraging. We opened a bank account.

Hard work, perseverance, determination and the ability to learn on the fly, those were the ingredients in our recipe for success.

Note: There are, of course, those in the government who work diligently, tirelessly, and not without personal sacrifice, on behalf of Moldova and its people, and many of them have, over the years, become vocal supporters of our work in Rîşcani..

Chapter Four

Up and Running, but Where?

'Begin at the beginning' is popular advice, and relatively easy to follow. But now, with MAD-Aid up and running, the question was: Where was it supposed to go? What comes after the beginning?

Well, the first item on our list—our short-term mission statement, you might say—was to collect things from U.K. hospitals at take them to Moldova. I divided this statement into its component parts and made a list:

1. Identify NIH hospitals we could work with—preferably within easy driving distance.
2. Find out who the decision-makers were at these hospitals, specifically, who was responsible for disposing of discarded furniture and equipment
3. Arrange a meeting with these decision-makers and convince them to donate these items to MAD-Aid
4. Arrange for collection of the donated items
5. Arrange for storage of these items until such time as enough were collected to constitute a full lorry load
6. Find qualified drivers to drive the lorry to Moldova
7. Make sure all the necessary paperwork, permits, etc., from the U.K., the E.U. and Moldova, were in place and all legitimate fees paid
8. Identify the Moldovan hospitals or institutions that would be recipients of the goods in this first shipment
9. Arrange for time off work to accompany the shipment to Moldova

I didn't set about to tackle each item on the list in order, just to make sure they were all done. So the first challenge I decided to take on—because I had an idea it would be easiest—was storage. Luckily, a farm managed by my Moldovan friend, Ruslan, was just coming to the end of its season so they had plenty of space and kindly offered us storage for free—until the next season.

Being able to cross off one of the items on my list was a big shot in the arm for me. Though my decision to solve the short-term storage problem first had been pure serendipity, I realize in retrospect that it was the best move I could have made. My advice to anyone embarking on a project, large or small, is to do the easy things first. Each success will not only bring your vision closer to reality, it will encourage you and give you the focus you need to identify and take the next step.

With storage in place, we had to work out where to get the donations from, so I went and spoke to the local hospital on the Isle of Wight and they were very keen to get involved. In fact, they were so enthusiastic that we signed a contract with them and arranged to take delivery of some of their surplus equipment in a few days.

Meanwhile, with Ann's help, we wrote a few letters to other hospitals in the South of England asking for their assistance.

Storage? Check.

Donations? Check

I decided the next step was to figure out how to get the aid to Moldova. Always nagging at me, when I considered this challenge, was the refrain I had heard over and over again, that it would be impossible to get through border bureaucracy. So there I was, working 40-60 hours per week at the hospital and, in my spare time, trying to come up with a way to get through the border once we got there.

Of course, that problem was academic if we couldn't raise the money we need to hire a lorry. The British transport firms I was talking to were extremely expensive, and none seemed anxious to take on a trip to Moldova, 'Wherever that is'.

Suddenly the items on my list weren't so easy to tick off. Here was the first challenge that seemed insurmountable: no transport, let alone enough money to pay for it. However, after hours and hours of research, I found a forwarder from Moldova who offered to take the shipment at a reasonable price. They also gave me guidance on packing and so on. However as soon as they realised that it was humanitarian aid, they directed my attention to a clause in contract stating that if the truck was held at the border for longer than 24 hours because of missing paperwork, we would be fined for each day's delay. And it was a hefty fine; too big a risk with our limited budget.

Back to the computer, where I started researching charities working in Moldova, and was surprised and pleased to find not one, but three operating from the U.K.

TEECH - Telecommunications Eastern European Challenge
Moldova AID Project
Child AID

By this time, word about MAD-Aid and the research I had conducted in Moldova, had spread quickly. That's how I first met Alexandru. His parents heard about what we were doing and contacted my mother to ask if she thought we could help them get a wheelchair for their nine year-old son who was housebound by his disabilities.

John and I immediately began scouring the island for wheelchairs and, in the course of our search, visited the Red Cross who suggested we go to Island Mobility. That's where

If TEECH can do it; so can I!

we met owner Rob Horton, who has since become one of MAD-Aid's key players. At the time, he said that he couldn't promise anything, but that he'd see what he could come up with.

A few days later, we got the call to come and collect not one, but two children's wheelchairs! So, through our contacts in Moldova, we identified another child, five year-old Igor, who needed one as well.

Now, all we had to do was get the wheelchairs to Moldova, 1500 miles and five countries away!

Through my research, I knew that TEECH had already been working for seven years in Moldova, and I discovered that a trip was planned that winter to deliver shoeboxes to orphanages and at-risk children. Then, the following summer, they were going to return with group of British volunteers to install toilets in Moldovan village schools—most of which had only outhouses to serve that purpose, extremely dangerous, especially in winter, and very unhygienic.

So I contacted TEECH Director Rob Brown and told him about my dilemma. TEECH not only agreed to take the wheelchairs, they delivered them to my Mum's doorstep! Rob also gave me the contact details for Ora International, the local NGO who helped them with border paperwork.

Foremost in the back of my mind, when the chairs had been delivered, was, 'It *can* be done! If TEECH can get through the border and deliver aid successfully, so can I!'

About that time, we went to visit the Moldova AID Project in Axminster, Essex. The charity, which has since ceased operations, had stopped sending aid to Moldova in 2010 because of border challenges, corruption, and bureaucracy. Their trustees gave us great advice and some items left over from their last mission.

Next, by calling every charity I found that worked in Moldova and seeking their advice, I got in contact with Martin Wilcox, manager of Child AID and found that for them, too, finding transport was a huge problem. As was finding the funds to pay for it.

Child AID has worked in Moldova for many years, and they fully support the Tony Hawks Centre that was set up by British comedian Tony Hawks to care for children with cerebral palsy. I explained to Martin what we intended to do and that we already have storage full of aid that we aiming to donate to Moldovan hospitals. Martin told me that he had visited the Mother and Child Hospital in the Capital, Chişinău, and he knew how bad the conditions were there. He said any help we could give to that hospital was desperately needed and would be greatly appreciated. Finally, he promised to think about how we could work together, and to ask his trustees for a donation.

Together with all of this, plus my full-time job, we staged three fund-raising events on the Isle of Wight:

- A launch evening for the charity.
- A 1940s night, which was a great success for the local community and for MAD-Aid.
- Our first ever Charity Ball, which was to become an annual event.
-

Slowly we were getting closer to meeting our goal of raising the funds needed to send our first truckload of aid, and really Making A Difference, in Moldova.

Child Aid came back with a large donation as well. And Sean Colson, one of our trustees ingeniously thought of selling logo space on the truck to sponsors from the Island. Sponsoring company's logos would travel with the aid all across Europe and into Moldova.

Wheels to the world!

Aid comes in all shapes and sizes

Chapter Five

Equipment

The difference between a dreamer and a visionary is that a dreamer just dreams. A visionary is willing to do the hard work it takes to make their dreams come true.

I invite you to imagine for a second the conditions in a Moldovan hospital. You have been brought in ill, so the last thing you care about is what bed you'll be in, as long as you get treatment, pain relief, and assurance that everything is fine. But then a wire from your broken bed frame pokes through your mattress, increasing your discomfort and pain.

Your surgery is just finished, and automatically, for no reason at all, you're taken on the same stretcher into ITU (called *reanimare* in Moldova). By now, the pain is worse as the anesthetic has worn off, so they decide to bring you back to the ward, where your bed is about one meter lower than the stretcher, and neither of them move up or down. You're in pain, and discomfort from your surgery, and now someone has to physically lift and lower you to the bed.

This is just a prelude of things to come. The patient's primary task is, first, to recover from the surgery, and second, to survive the aftercare.

Now imagine you're the parent or child of a hospitalized patient, that you have to stand by helplessly and witness their pain and discomfort and, perhaps worst of all, the negligence and carelessness that is a legacy of Soviet-era medical care. Imagine your frustration to watch them strapped to ancient metal-frame gurneys, in which they're wheeled to rusted beds, placed on filthy mattresses, covered with stained sheets and blankets, in cramped, unhygienic wards that are served by inadequate sanitary facilities.

That's what I go through every time my Mum or another loved one needs medical attention. It's not medical care, it's a parody, a tragic-comedy acted by imbeciles. I hate the memory of the unheeded cries of pain, the appalling smell of sickness that permeates the air, the decrepit facilities that seem to turn to dust even as you stare at them.

It is that memory, however, that fueled my determination to create MAD-Aid, and bring about change— even if only little change—in the Moldovan health care system. It is that memory that made me deaf to those who said, 'it can't be done'.

They still say it.

I'm still as deaf.

With the wheelchairs and clothing, we had proven that getting aid from the U.K. to Moldova was feasible. As a result, the lives of two young boys had been changed forever for the better! True, it was only a tiny step, but it gave us great confidence. It *could* be done. We had done it! Now all we needed to do was streamline the process, and take on bigger challenges.

That led to our next priority: the transfer of a whole hospital's worth of unneeded or surplus equipment, furniture and supplies from the U.K. to Moldova. As events unfolded, this vision was modified to target the refurbishment of the cardiology ward in Rîşcani hospital. The second step toward realization of our grand vision was under way!

However, confidence being an ephemeral commodity, I was worried: would I have enough donations to make the trip worthwhile? Where would I get the funds to do it? What if, like so many said, we'd never be able to make it through the border? I'm pretty sure that everyone has doubts at different stages in their life. As I write, I'm reminded of one of John's many great stories about crossing the border, this time in a car.

John's a kid at heart, and loves singing toys. On his first trip to Moldova, he noticed that the children had very little or nothing like that. So, even before we started the charity, when he came across a huge post-Christmas sale of singing toys in a shop, he bought about 20 of them!

As we were taking them to Moldova, the border guard came and said, 'Hold on! You can't take more than two items per person if they are new.' John started arguing that they were not new, but the border man wouldn't have it. So John took them all out of their boxes, put them all down in the Border car park and started them. So there they were, all twenty toys dancing, singing, clapping, and making a huge noise! 'There. Now they're used,' John said. The customs people just gaped at him, then at the dancing toys, then at one another and, finally, unable to think of anything else, shrugged and let us go.

I have hundreds of similar stories.

Anyway, back to my story: We started collecting equipment. The Isle of Wight Hospital came on board and soon we became their best friends. The Red Cross also gave us their equipment.

The Isle of Wight, where we live, is very much a community and word spreads quickly. Before we could turn around, the local hospice contacted us with a donation of fourteen hydraulic beds. Then the floodgates opened! The aid started arriving so fast we were quickly running out of storage space.

Ever since, we've never been short of donations.

At the time, though, as John and I and a few volunteers were still the only people collecting the donations, we had to refuse so much. It was extremely hard for me to say 'no'; it is still now, but I am learning I have to. We were given everything from hospital beds to a complete dental surgery, school furniture, hospital bedside lockers, bedding, clothing and wheelchairs. The list is endless.

By this time, several people had donated storage space, but some of them were getting nervous because of the sheer volume of items we were receiving; their space was filling much faster than they'd expected. You may think that I was excited by this amazing outpouring of generosity—and I was—but with every day the task became more daunting. I still had my day job at the hospital, and now I had to divide my remaining hours between collecting and sorting donations, fundraising, logistics, and the pile of paperwork associated with shipping. We also followed the aid every step of the way to its final destination: the people in need. We still do, but this became more and more demanding as the volume of deliveries increased.

With the transport forwarder and our trustees, we arranged the date for loading the first truck. Every evening we counted and re-counted the donations, making sure everything was correct and compliant with border procedures, and all the paperwork was complete with all the 'i's dotted and 't's crossed. After much thought and deliberation, we decided that the aid would be divided between the Mother and Child Hospital, and the trauma ward and Cardiology Ward in Rîşcani Hospital. Other aid such as wheelchairs, crutches and clothes would be delivered to individual recipients.

To sort all the paperwork for customs clearance, and learn how to do it properly was an interesting experience. I started by asking for advice from the Moldova Embassy in London. They kindly gave me the whole list of papers needed—about 30+ sheets for each truck, half from U.K. government departments and half from Moldovan. I also contacted the manager at Ora International and she kindly agreed to do help us with our paperwork.

Ora International was a local NGO, part of German charity chain. They have been delivering aid for many years, and were able to guide us for our very first shipment.

The Moldovan Embassy gave me the contact details for the person responsible for issuing the authorization for humanitarian aid. Of course, since I was a complete novice, I had all sorts of questions. I must have sent this person about 5-6 mails, to each of which he responded promptly and politely. I was surprised, therefore, when Mariana Botnari, who was to become the Manager of Moldova Aid, our Moldovan partner charity, went to submit the originals and apply for authorization, he said I'd sent him so many mails, it was as though we are relatives!

This first delivery trip was a test, because I knew it would make or break the charity. If, after all our effort, something went wrong, people on both ends of the delivery chain would lose confidence in me. I worried about customs clearance; I worried about demands for bribes, which I refused to pay. I worried about the famous statement that in Moldova all the Aid is sold. I worried about the weather. I worried about the air pressure in the truck tires! My brain was a worry machine working overtime!

At last, the day came when the truck was loaded and sent off. As a team, we all worked very efficiently. The drivers, especially, being Romanian themselves, were very helpful. They knew how urgently this aid was needed, so they were as excited as we were, but just as worried, too, since they'd never carried humanitarian aid before, only commercial goods. Who knew what regulatory adventures lay in store? This was new territory.

Also the farm manager, Ruslan Ciobanu, and his team were great. We also had a visit from the local newspaper, as in their view this was a great project for the Island. British people inherit a charitable spirit from a young age, and it's passed down from generation to generation. They are very open to helping those less fortunate and take great pleasure in doing so.

On our own time and with our own money, John and I decided to fly to Moldova to meet the truck and make sure aid arrived safely and was distributed in accordance with our trustees' expectations.

Not so fast!

When John, our Treasurer, tried to pay the invoice and transfer the money to the transport company the transfer wouldn't go through. He tried again the next day. Still no luck. Why? I didn't know then, and I don't know now. What I did know was that we had to get a shipment of aid to Moldova, so I asked the transport company if I could simply bring cash since I would be in Moldova before the truck and was told that would be no problem.

So, with 3500 euros in hand, we arrived at the transport company office to pay for the shipment. Then the ugly head of Moldovan bureaucracy raised its head. 'To pay cash, you need to prove where the money came from.' Well I had more than enough proof in my view, but not theirs. Two long days and many frustrating phone calls later, we finally agreed on a way the company would accept our cash. Why? Even today I don't have a clue. John was concerned. If the transport company couldn't legally take our cash, could they legally deliver the aid? This was just first hurdle.

We went to the border to meet the truck, and there it was!

A hundred feet and two centuries separate Romania and Moldova. As we sorted through the paperwork the customs agent discovered a stamp missing on one item. Then a duplicate permit. Then...

The truck had arrived at the border at 7:00 a.m. John and I had arrived at 8 a.m. We were still there at 5:30 in the afternoon. We'd spent most of the intervening hours pacing around the truck, thinking the worst, and getting nervous, then frustrated, then angry. Frankly, there came a time, about mid-afternoon, when we looked at each other and said, 'Well if we get stuck, we just leave the Aid here and be finished with Moldova.'

It was the 7th of March, the day before International Women's Day, a bank holiday in Moldova. Because the working day was shorter, in preparation for the holiday, we began to suspect that the truck might be held up for another three days, but luckily we crossed the border by 17.30.

The next task was unloading. Our spirits had recovered somewhat by the time we arrived at the Mother and Child Hospital, but were dashed once we were told that they couldn't receive the aid because those responsible—the accountant and the storekeeper—had gone home at 2:00 that afternoon and there was no one to sign for the delivery. 'Please come back on Monday, as nothing can be done'.

Okay. So there we were in Chişinău, on the eve of a national holiday, having to look for storage space to unload and store the aid for a few days while the rest of the truck carried on to Rîşcani with aid for the second hospital? Our first call was to Ora International and, fortunately, they had space in their store. We unloaded the aid yet to be delivered to Mother and Child Hospital and began the drive to Rîşcani. The truck drivers were Romanian, and joked that the holes in the road were so deep, they lost their mobile phone signal each time their tyres hit one!

It was 10:30 p.m. by the time we arrived at Rîşcani, but everyone was waiting. The ward's lead doctor and her family, the staff and the patients and our own volunteers—mainly my friends and family—were all waiting to help unload! I can't begin to tell you, after all we'd been through, and how exhausted we were, how heartening this welcome was!

We unloaded the truck within an hour and left to rest, agreeing to come back to sort out the paper work after the bank holiday. Meanwhile, we visited a few disabled people, especially children, delivering wheelchairs.

The weather was wet, and the roads so muddy, we struggled to drive to some houses and walking proved extremely difficult. We began to wonder how much use a wheelchair would be on roads like this.

The bank holiday and weekend passed, and we went back to Rîşcani Hospital and found the old beds and bedside lockers out and the new ones in. We saw the joy in the ward staff's eyes and caught snatches of patient's comments as we passed through the halls: 'These are the people who brought the TV in our room!' 'Those are the ones who brought the new beds!'

However, while we were having a cup of coffee and talking with ward's lead doctor, the accountant turned up and started fussing because we hadn't waited for him before deciding how to distribute the items!

John found it funny, I was quite upset, so we went to head of the hospital and made it clear our plan was to fully address the needs of one ward at a time. That way we could demonstrate clear improvements to our supporters back in the U.K., which would ensure the continued flow of aid necessary to outfit the rest of the hospital. We said that the cardiology ward was going to be done first and that the furniture is there to stay, not to be scattered throughout the hospital.

Some people weren't very happy with this arrangement as they wanted to use the equipment to fix up a VIP room in every ward, but there was nothing they could do.

A sense of hopelessness descended upon John and me when, our mission completed, we drove back to my village, to my mother's house. After long, thoughtful, troubled silence, John said, 'Victoria, this is beyond us. We can't really make a difference. The mission is huge! I think we should just go back home, thank people for their help and say, 'Look, we tried. We did our best, but, in the end, there's nothing we can do.' We need to stop this madness and carry on with our lives. We don't have the time or the finances to carry on.'

I hung my head. He was right. I felt helpless in the light of what we had discovered in the hospitals. All our work hadn't even scratched the surface. How *could* we carry on? How do we identify what is most important? How could we bring about real change in the face of such overwhelming need, government indifference, bureaucratic interference and archaic treatment paradigms? Thousands of bitter questions stumbled over one another in my mind, but no answers. 'Okay,' I said.

John wanted to be out of Moldova. He couldn't help but be upset at the contrast between all the Porsches and Ferraris around Chişinău and the decrepit, filthy beds in the children's hospital in the same city.

Before we left, we decided that we would make one last visit to see Alexandru, the child who received a wheelchair from us, delivered a few months earlier by TEECH. He lives in the village of Mihaileni, where I was born.

As adults, you would think that once we'd decided something we would stick to it, but not us! Once the cardiology ward in Rîşcani had been outfitted and set up, we returned to the Mother and Child Hospital in Chişinău and saw the aid been delivered there. This was more than a shocking experience. Conditions were much worse than we had seen in Bălţi or Rîşcani. A nurse said to me that last summer they took the beds out washed them with petrol to take the rust off! We're talking about a children's hospital, about the future generation and their well-being. As I looked into the sad eyes of the parents who had no choice but to put their children through this experience, I was reminded of a time when I was young that I came to this place for treatment.

I remembered it being slightly better, but that was 20 years ago and nothing had changed since.

When we arrived, Alexandru and his family were waiting for us, wanted to feed us—as every family in Moldova does. Alexandru was animated. He talked excitedly about everything. Then he got into his wheelchair and his dad took him outside.

We were just about to leave, when Alexandru looked at John—no doubt thinking that, as a foreigner, he must be the one who had given him the wheelchair—and with wide, innocent eyes said, 'Thank you very much for my wheelchair. Now I can come out here and breathe the air. I can feel the sun. I can see the trees, not just the leaves that scrape my bedroom window.'

John couldn't understand a word, but he didn't have to. The look in Alexandru's eyes, and the tone of his voice made him choke up. Nevertheless, I translated Alexandru's words and of course, that brought a tear to our eyes. As we were walking back to my mum's house, John stopped and took my hand and said: 'Victoria, it's hard, but we have choices. Many of them don't! So let's not stop, not as long as we can help someone!'

'Confused' didn't begin to describe my feelings, our feelings.

That visit gave us perspective. We didn't have to save Moldova. We had to save Alexandru, and the next Alexandru, and the next. And each Alexandru we saved, represented a family whose life was, in ways large and small, lifted from despair.

If we could dress one more family in warm clothes against the winter blast; if we could outfit one home with proper windows or running water; if we could provide one child with sufficient food, with medical care, we *would* have Made a Difference! And if we could manage to finish refurbishing that cardiology ward, more than 300 patients a year would have a better chance at full recovery!

So that was it. We decided we were *not* going to stop. The question was how do we go about carrying on?

Back in U.K., I became the ultimate multi-tasker. While doing my ironing at home, I would listen to TED talks. I still do. During one TED talk, Daniel Ally said that books have all the information we need to solve all the problems in the world. I'm not sure I agree with that, but I figured there *were* books that would help us solve *our* problems, or at least point us in the right direction, and help us ask the right questions, and those were the only books I had to read.

During my break hour at the hospital, I started reading about what other charities were doing, how they tackled the problems, and achieved their aims.

But, despite the experience of the last couple of years, I was reaching a level where everything was new. I was starting in a very complex new field with limited time, limited finances, and I had a lot of catching up to do.

The good thing is that I was never alone. I always had my husband and my faithful trustees, and I leaned on them often. Every time we met, I left with a clearer vision of what MAD-Aid was, and what we could accomplish through it. These people need medals! They were dealing not just with my inexperience, but with the fact that I'm a very impulsive person, and want everything done yesterday. My tendency is to take on a fistful of projects at once—and this just fueled my desire to respond to all the requests for aid now pouring in from Moldova.

Getting that first truckload of aid to Moldova taught me several things: first, that I needed a Moldovan NGO partner, one that would operate with the same aims, agenda, values, and principals. Together, we would have to put systems in place that assured transparency and accountability were at acceptable levels. I had to learn not just how to set up a proper U.K. charity, but also a Moldova one. Originally we thought the Moldovan organization would be a subdivision of MAD-Aid, but it became clear that it was easier to open a separate partner organization, also run by volunteers. My family in Moldova stepped in, not because they understood what I was trying to do, just because they respected my wishes, and wanted to help. And so Moldova Aid, our partner, was born.

Now I needed a manager I could trust. So again I relied on a family member, Mariana Botnari, to step in. She was at home with no employment at that time, so she kindly agreed to do all the registration of documents and run the organization as volunteer.

Mariana Botnari with Vadim, Phoenix' official Director of Welcome

All the while, donations were coming in, almost uncontrollably, and we needed new storage, more volunteers! The need remains. Even today, every single donated item stored by and delivered through MAD-Aid is collected by John and me and a few of our friends. Still, we managed to send over 200 tonnes of aid from the Isle of Wight, every ounce of which, at one time or another, passed through John's hands.

By that time, we were getting phone calls from hospitals right across the U.K., offering us valuable donations—equipment and material that could change lives back in Moldova—but our financial resources were too small to allow us to work further afield than the Isle of Wight and Southampton.

One day the person at the other end of the phone line told me that she was responsible for the Devon NHS area and asked me if I could collect 3000 hydraulic/electrical hospital beds. Three thousand of them! 50 truckloads! Enough to replace all the beds in the Mother and Child hospital, leaving no rusty ones. But we couldn't fund the transport. We even tried to see if the Moldovan government could pay for the transport. We needed £150 000—£50 per bed. But we were too young as charity and even raising £3000 was a struggle.

To have to decline such a generous offer broke my heart.

The idea of sending one truck per year was slowly going out of window along with our original concept for the charity. In June, just three months after our first load, we were ready to ship another one, but we were still not close to having the funds to pay for it. However, the storage needed to be emptied so some of the trustees came and helped pack the second load. This included hospital equipment, complete dental surgeries, and much more.

The Trustees and I tried our best to see our way forward, but everyone had limited spare time. I transferred to the night shift at the hospital. It was the only way I could continue to do the charity work pretty much full time.

Today, on average, we send four trucks per year from MAD-Aid to Moldova. And when the resources aren't available to get shipments to Moldova, we send them to

Romania, Belarus, Ukraine and Africa—wherever we find partners able to pay for transport.

Of course, wherever this aid ends up—in Moldova or elsewhere—it transforms people's lives. The satisfaction of playing a part in that can't be measured in economic terms.

Chapter Six

Mobility to Ability

Like most isolated communities, the Isle of Wight can seem an insular, quirky place. If you do something right, word gets around very quickly. The same holds true if you do something wrong—except perhaps a little more quickly.

We got a phone call from the Isle of Wight prison; the inmates were repairing broken wheelchairs—doing them up so nicely, even adding toy cars and camouflage paint jobs for boys' wheelchairs, and flowers and dolls for the girls' wheelchairs—and they wanted us to have them!

By this time, we were also taking delivery of wheelchairs from the Southampton hospice and the Red Cross—together with other medical equipment and furniture—which we delivered to World War II veterans and disabled adults in Moldova who had given up hoping for such a miracle. We also served children with disabilities, but until the call from the prison, we only had few here and there. So here was a new opportunity.

Some say the Age of Miracles is past. I'd have to be blind to subscribe to that point of view.

Things like this keep happening when you least expect them to; and they happen for a reason. Within a month we had around 200 wheelchairs. My eyes lit up, spotless and shining in the afternoon light, nearly new! I thought here, in one fell swoop, we can change 200 lives!

Sometimes I surprise even myself with how naïve I can be.

At our next trustee meeting, I asked permission to send these new wheelchairs to Moldova in time for Disability Day on 3rd of December, and to go along to host a small concert to which I could bring all these disabled children together and offer them a wheelchair. I didn't want to just distribute the chairs to their homes but, especially, to bring them together to show them that they're not alone, to show them that the wheelchair could broaden the horizons of their world, to connect them to life beyond their doors, outside their four walls. There are lots of children like them, with same conditions, the same infirmities, the same struggles.

If I were to accomplish this, I'd have to get the wheelchairs on the June delivery—the last before Christmas—which meant I had just six weeks to pull everything together! As if the simple logistics weren't enough, MAD-Aid still owed the trustees for the last transport. So their directive was clear: If I managed to raise the money owed and, over-and-above that, enough to send the June shipment, then they'd agree to it. My suspicion was that they thought it was impossible but, by this time, they'd also learned they were dealing with a madwoman!

I took three or four days off work, and started from scratch, making phone calls, sending emails, and going back to Community Action Isle of Wight for more advice. Slowly, slowly I was getting closer, but not close enough. I needed around £7000 to repay the loan and send the shipment; for a small charity with no proper network yet, that was daunting amount of money.

By this time I had developed a real friendship with Tudorel Moraru (Doru), manager of the transport company, who later became strong supporter of MAD-Aid. He offered me a deal: half a load at a greatly reduced rate! Still, the loan had to be repaid, so I went back to the trustees and, being very supportive and understanding, they allowed me to delay repayment of the loan so we could afford to send the shipment.

The wheelchair shipment was becoming a reality!

It was a hard day's work for all of us who loaded the truck. We were unable to park next to the storage facility because the access road was too narrow. So, we moved all the wheelchairs from storage to the truck by van. (You've heard the saying 'two is always better than one?' Not so when it comes to moves required to load a truck!) Despite the hard work, our spirits were high; we were a good team and it was great to see all those wheelchairs on their way! We were especially thankful for the drivers who always pitched in to help. They made the job so much easier, and much of our success rode on their shoulders.

After loading the truck, I still had a small mountain of paperwork to sort out. So did Mariana on the other end, in Moldova. Driving back home extremely tired, I was not looking forward to sitting at the computer for the next few hours. But at home I had a surprise: a cheque for £3750 had arrived from a grant application I had made during my few days off. Sometimes good luck is the result of sheer, dogged persistence. I never stopped applying for grants. Most of the time nothing came of it, but sometimes . . .

It was an amazing feeling; the wheelchairs could actually be on their way! MAD-Aid started thinking about a place in Moldova to celebrate their distribution. First, we asked Doru, the owner of the transport company, and who also owns a few production companies making clothes for U.K. high street shops, if he would sponsor the event in Moldova, by paying for the venue and food, and he agreed.

We hoped the Social Services would pay for transporting the beneficiaries to the venue. Toward that end, I asked the Minister of the Social Protection agency, CREPOR, which was responsible for providing wheelchairs for people with disabilities, for a list of people waiting for their first wheelchair. And here was another rude awakening: the list contained 1800 names! And, at that, the information only included the name, address, and when they became disabled. That was it. When combined with the separate list of potential recipients we had compiled from our previous visits, we realized the immensity of the need, and our inability to meet it with our existing resources.

I should note that, despite the size of the official list, many were not on it. I was to learn the reason later: in order to be included on the list, the applicant was required to make two or three trips to their doctor, then to Social Services, then—providing they get Social Service approval—to Chisinău to complete the application process. Of course, with no transport, no money, and no wheelchair this task was pretty much impossible for those most in need.

Nevertheless, the list kept getting longer.

Apparently, Moldova never produced or bought a wheelchair since its independence, relying solely on donations. And of course, because these come from different places, different countries, and different organizations, there is no standardization, nor was there any system in place to keep track of them.

Ministry for Social Protection - Chisinău

Eventually we decided to have the event in Bălţi in order to be more central, and be able to include more disabled people, and to begin to keep better records.

The shipment was on its way. We had selected a venue in Bălţi from which to celebrate the distribution of the wheelchairs. Now it only remained for Social Services to transport to the venue as many beneficiaries as we were able to handle.

I expected them to jump at the chance to provide this vital equipment—*free* equipment—to those of their constituents whose needs were officially recognized. Not so. There is, in the mindset of the average Moldovan bureaucrat, the residue of Soviet socialism that stands resolutely in the path of change of any kind, which seems to consider it their sole purpose to prevent rather than facilitate progress. And now it reared its granite head. We were told that all the potential recipients were bed-bound and, therefore, couldn't be safely transported to the venue.

I knew this was not the case. It was simply that the government chose to *define* many disabled children as bed-bound. This designation released the government from any obligation to care for them beyond the absolute minimum to keep them alive. To be perfectly fair, though, the designation is not entirely without merit.

Moldova does not have a single occupational therapist, so when Social Services say someone is bed-bound, they are, to some extent, correct. The list of equipment that could free children and adults with disabilities from the prison of their beds and let them be more independent: hoists, bath support bars, bath seats, bath lifts, sliding sheets, banana boards, standing aids, walking aids, ramps, picking tools and so much more, are virtually unknown in Moldova, even today.

Still, I was furious to hear children as young as three or four labeled bed-bound, simply to get them off the list that would entitle them to the care they deserved! I knew that they didn't *have* to be bed-bound; these were real, vital people with active minds and vivid imaginations, trapped in damaged bodies, bodies that, with proper care, nutrition, and therapy might be made useful servants to those active minds.

I *knew* that. I worked in the same sector in the U.K., and I knew that it was very rare—beyond cases of terminal illness, or in the most extreme instances—for disabled people to be permanently bed-bound.

At last, however, despite the obstacles that seemed to keep cropping up on our path, we persisted, managing to bring together about seventy children and adults for the presentation of the wheelchairs. The British Ambassador, Phillip Batson, who had been an early and enthusiastic advocate of the project, was present, as were the Moldovan Ministers of Labour, Social Protection and Family, and the deputy Minister of Health.

At the event, I was shocked—though I shouldn't have been, had I thought about it—to realize that, for many of the recipients, this was the first time they'd ever seen other disabled children—many, many of them. This was mind-blowing for them! Prior to that, most lived in such isolation that they imagined they were totally alone in their affliction.

It also became apparent that many adults saw their disabled child not as the unique, precious individual he or she was, but as a burden that, from a purely practical standpoint, they were. For families whose every effort, every penny, had to go toward putting food on the table at day's end, a non-contributing member *is* a burden. There were fears among family members, I suspect, that any degree of mobility would just compound the burden, rather than relieve it.

Surveying the situation that day, as each child was settled in his or her wheelchair, I might have agreed with them. Most were used to being shunted out of the way and more or less ignored. Rather than the happy, smiling faces I had, frankly, anticipated, they just sat—rather slumped there, clueless as to where they were, why they were there, or what was happening to them—let alone knowing what to do or how to use the chair.

I had to remind myself that, in human terms, nobody must be considered a burden. Over and over again, history had shown that, once a segment of society takes it upon themselves to determine the worthiness of another, disaster follows.

These were children. Human beings. Not invalids.

It was a powerful and moving celebration. I watched, almost in disbelief, as a man entered carrying his 34-year-old brother in a sack! Each case was unique and pretty much all of them needed not just a wheelchair, but therapy to bring life to atrophied muscles so the chair would be useful. Until then, it was just fancy furniture.

I made three mental notes: First, together with wheelchairs, we would need to provide training in how to adjust, repair, service and maintain them in peak working order. Second, we had to match each chair to its end-user and, third, we had to provide for the physical needs of the end-user in order strengthen them enough to make use of the chair to their greatest advantage.

For the first point, we had a proven model to follow: we had followed the chairs through the refurbishment process from beginning to end. For the most part things just needed modernizing, updating, and routine maintenance. For the second point, somehow a system would need to be put in place that would track our efforts to find disabled people, including those of whom none but their families were aware, defining their need and matching it with our resources. The last, though, preparing people with disabilities to use the wheelchairs, was uncharted territory. Under the Soviet system, disabled citizens had been marginalized nearly to the point of invisibility, and very little had changed since.

I now saw that it wasn't enough just to provide a wheelchair; we needed to understand the child, their need, their limitations, desires, and potential. I began to think: What does a wheelchair actually *do* for a disabled child? Of course, it can get them out of the house, if they're lucky and the roads and weather permit. In many instances, it would allow parents or caregivers to wheel the child to the hospital, maybe to the market, or church, even, possibly, to school—or a job!

Most importantly, it could give them the mobility to participate in the life of their community.

For me, the event revealed a big problem; we had done the equivalent of turning up with a truck full of shoes and giving everyone a random pair without regard to size, stride, weight, or need. Yes, we had brought 200 chairs, but they had been distributed, more or less, randomly. In other words, we had brought some wonderful tools, but they weren't necessarily fit to the needs of their user.

Awaiting Repair

Much of the problem, once again, lay with the State. Beyond names and addresses, they kept no record of the disabled children, nothing to signify their specific need, or any of the personal information that would make it possible for us to more perfectly match a chair to a child.

With mixed emotions, with so many more surreal situations, with questions reproducing like rabbits in my mind, the day drew to a close. I was struck, once again, how British I had become. My thinking no longer focused helplessly on problems, but on solutions.

Where to start?

That same November, when we held the wheelchair distribution event, the British Ambassador organized a conference for all the British charities working in Moldova. There I met organizations like Lumos, who were trying to implement, introduce, and promote social inclusion. They managed to help formulate legislation for inclusive education—an important step in the right direction.

The UN Convention for the Rights of People with Disabilities had been ratified by the Moldovan parliament in 2012, another step forward. But ratification and implementation are two different things. How can inclusive education be enacted when it's not clear how many children are affected, what disabilities they have, what equipment and additional resources they need, and what educational, counseling, and personal support they require?

What I knew from launching the charity was that we wanted to give children with disabilities the same opportunities as anyone else: to restore to them the right to a full and productive life of which they had been deprived by society, by endemic poverty, as well as by the legal system and government that should have been their champion.

When I came to the U.K. for the second time in 2006, my Lithuanian friend and I used to joke that in our country we didn't have disabled people because we ate natural food, grown in the garden by ourselves. England has so many disabled people because they were eating fish and chips. Around the streets you would see so many people with special needs just living a normal life. This was a joke for us.

The reality, I came to learn, was that the Soviet mentality that was still a part of Moldovan DNA, didn't count people with disabilities as people. Rather than serve them, the official response was to keep them out of sight and, therefore, out of mind. In fact, under that draconian system, which was in effect within recent memory, it was against the law to hire a disabled individual! *Disabled—burden to society!* was an official Soviet slogan

The prejudice, stereotyping, and negative attitude towards people with special needs still require aggressive revision. Accessibility—in the form of roads, ramps, and equipment for these people—requires much investment and a change of approach. Additionally, certificates of disability must be conferred only upon those correctly and verifiably diagnosed as medically and/or psychologically impaired.

But even more urgent, to me, was the need for the creation of an accurate database of affected people. How could we develop effective services for them without reliable data upon which to base our decisions? How could we provide and distribute the correct equipment without knowing exactly what type was needed?

So...

In 2016 we started to build a small database of citizens with special needs aged 5-35. A group of evaluators, each consisting of an able-bodied person and a disabled person, has been trained to evaluate a person with special needs from the perspective of offering independence, as well as the necessary services that will lead to social inclusion. An important part of the training is achieving familiarity with all the equipment available in U.K.

Once again, as the statistics mounted, we were shocked by the results. These people needed much more than a wheelchair. They needed proper nutrition and a hygienic environment. They needed indoor plumbing and reliable electric service. Their homes had to be made handicap-friendly. Most importantly, they needed the education, inclusion, and medical care that would allow them to be, to the best of their ability, productive citizens.

We have compiled case notes for every single person and, now, we have begun to address the needs of each. Already, we have found partial solutions for many of them. Providing *complete* solutions is possible, but will require the active involvement by parents or caregivers, as well as the determination of local authorities, central authorities, donors, churches, relief organizations, to tackle the challenges of providing for Moldova's disabled population. Who knows how many Helen Kellers, Steven Hawkings, or Stevie Wonders may be hidden among them?

Peace Corps worker James Buchanan with Oleg Slobodeau

It's time to break the barriers, to open the boxes and remove the labels. It's time to see the child, and not their wheelchair, their potential and not their disability.

Chapter Seven

The Power of Together

MAD-Aid has always been willing to learn from others and help others where possible. From the beginning, the charity started to work in partnership with other organizations. In our view, we can do so much more working together than individually. We don't work for us, we work for those who have so much less hope, to help them achieve their dreams and fulfill their potential.

At the beginning, while I was trying to find a way to transport our very first load of humanitarian aid, I came across the Communication Workers Union Humanitarian Aid, CWUHA. It is made up of 'trade unionists, families, and friends, who work in Britain's and Ireland's postal, telecom & financial industries (and who) respond to the plight of vulnerable children in other countries and the U.K. & Ireland.' This is a great organization with years of experience and a very successful track record. At the time I told them what we were trying to do, their plans were for convoys to Lithuania and Bulgaria for the next two years. They said there was no way they would go back into Moldova for a couple of reasons: First, because it was their intention to serve children on both sides of the Dneister river—in Moldova and separatist Transnistria—and because that was virtually impossible without spending valuable days at the borders.

NOTE: Though Transnistria is part of Moldova, it's divided from the rest of the country by a border it imposes, but which no other nation recognizes. The region has its own passports and currency, which again, no one apart from Russia recognize— whenever it's politically convenient. Since the civil war that created the semi-autonomous region in 1994, Russia has kept roughly 2000 troops in Transnistria, despite its international agreement to withdraw them by 2004. In fact, in the fall of 2016, 2000 more troops were added. With this foreign military, as well as Russian economic support, the region has its own de facto government, their own laws, and separate administrative authorities and ministries, the result being that any legal authority Chișinău has over them is on paper only.

Transnistra is the easternmost region of Moldova

What could I say? I was not able to offer any assurance even for Moldova, let alone Transnistria. At the time, everyone was advising me that taking aid into the country was impossible. We agreed to meet at some point, to learn more about each other's organizations, and left it at that.

About eighteen months later, I got a call from Mick Kirgby, a trustee of CWUHA, asking me to give a talk at their Annual General Meeting (AGM) in preparation for their 20th anniversary. Also, he asked to have a meeting with me, as they really would love to go back to Moldova. By this time I had learned that crossing the Moldovan border with humanitarian aid *was* possible, and not too bad providing all the paperwork is in order. I could start to negotiate travel back to Moldova and assure them that their aid would be safely delivered. Furthermore, the British Ambassador, charity representatives, and the head of the Customs department had a meeting and simplified the procedure considerably. And MAD-Aid/Moldova AID's policy of complete transparency resulted in our being put on Green Corridor list, which means far faster passage through border control and customs.

I was getting ready for the AGM presentation and talk, and very nervous as there would be more than fifty people in the room. I was talking in front of an organization with more experience taking aid to Moldova than I had. What was I going to tell them? I needed support. So, just as I had when all this began, I decided to ask John to come with me as really needed his support. He said yes. (I almost said that he said he'd be happy to go. But, well, he went).

Departure day arrived, and we went to Bournemouth to be met by a group of lovely CWUHA people. Everyone was so friendly, it seemed like we'd known each other for a long time.

The presentation went really well. I chose to talk more about Moldova than about MAD-Aid, but everyone was interested in MAD-Aid's work, so we started talking, and talking led to brain-storming. I came very close to getting CWUHA to agree to come back to Moldova for their 20th anniversary. After more meetings and explaining to them how border crossing had become easier, and agreeing that we would do all the paperwork, I managed to persuade the trustees to agree to do a trial run—four trucks of aid—to Moldova in May, 2015. The typical CWUHA convoy can be anything up to ten trucks.

MAD-Aid Convoy at the Moldovan Border

In November, 2014, two CWUHA trustees came to Moldova with me. We visited a hospital as well as a few families and, in the end, agreed to concentrate on helping four villages with aid for the most vulnerable families. We also agreed to support the Tony Hawke's Centre (one of the first centres in Moldova providing therapy for children with cerebral palsy). In addition, CWUHA would bring aid for children from Rîşcani Hospital Children's Ward and for the Oncology Hospital Children's Ward. We identified some of the most desperate families, created a list of their needs, and CWUHA drivers immediately began collecting donations and getting ready for the long trip to Moldova to fulfill the promise of their slogan: *Delivering Smiles to Needy Children*.

May was getting closer fast. We had sent eight trucks by then, but this time things were different: these were British drivers, volunteering their time and wanting to deliver aid personally. The last thing we wanted for them to be stopped at the border or get stuck in piles with paper.

Mariana, from Moldova AID, and I did all the paperwork, informed the British Ambassador and the head of Moldovan Customs control that the convoy would be arriving. And I recall as if it were yesterday being at the border waiting for the trucks to arrive and thinking, 'The next hour could destroy all I've done so far'. I knew with certainty that if we struggled at that border, the convoy would not return and I would lose my credibility.

At the Sculeni border crossing, there is only one lane for incoming traffic, which causes a bottleneck. A border control agent said I would be allowed to cross the border as soon as the trucks arrived on the other side. I asked him what we needed to do, given our Green Corridor status, to get the trucks through as quickly as possible. He said there was nothing we could do; the trucks would have to wait like everybody else.

Of course, his attitude, after all the hoops I had jumped through to get Green Corridor status, did not allay my concerns. Quite the opposite, so I asked to speak with the shift supervisor. Thankfully, he was extremely helpful and made room for the convoy to pass, dealt with paper work immediately, and everything went smoothly. All the trucks were out of customs clearance and border checks within two hours, which is pretty good for four fully loaded vehicles. From there, we drove to another customs clearance point where the trucks were checked, and, because all the aid and paperwork was correct, we were signaled through and headed for the hotel!

In front of us were four busy days of delivering aid.

We sorted the aid and delivered it to more people than I could count. I can't describe what a joy it was to witness the transformation as families accustomed to struggling to survive each day received not only thirty days worth of food, but microwaves and kettles to cook it with! We also provided clothes, school supplies, toys, hygienic products and more. There's nothing more fulfilling than making a positive difference in people's lives. I love it! But, to an extent, the process involves invading people's privacy; in order to meet needs, we had to know the needs, which meant that we witnessed real poverty, real desperation, and hopelessness. We were providing temporary relief. But we weren't coming up with solutions to the underlying problems.

That was to come later.

With British Ambassador Batson and wife, Jo, and CWUHA team at Tony Hawke's Centre, Chişinău

Toward the end of our stay, we visited the children's hospital in Rîşcani. The appalling conditions the drivers discovered there left them shocked and speechless, and underscored how badly the aid they brought was needed.

Next stop, the Tony Hawks centre in Chişinău. Together with CWUHA, we managed to provide most of their wish list as well, with specialised walking frames for children, sensory toys, nappies, wipes, a sensory chair, CWUHA Anniversary Teddies, now known as 'Tuzla Ted' and, of course, sweets. British Ambassador Phil Batson and his wife Jo, both active supporters of the Tony Hawks Centre, kindly turned out to help us unload and welcome us to Moldova.

When the last good-byes were said, we left the team at Moldova AID with a month's worth of aid still to be delivered! This was CWUHA's first convoy in partnership with us and it was, in the view of everyone who participated, a great success.

Many, many more truckloads followed the first, and continue to do so. And each has—in ways large and small—had a hand in transforming thousands of lives. Today, we continue to work closely with CWUHA, Child Aid, TEECH, Tony Hawkes, and many other British charities working in Moldova, and are profoundly grateful to all those who have caught the vision, and contributed so selflessly of their time, talents, and resources to make it a reality.

In partnership with CWUHA, and as a spin-off from the convoys, we also initiated a football tournament for kids called CWUHA Cup, providing all the equipment, kit, medals, and awards.

Another interesting partnership has been with Sandown Rotary Club from the Isle of Wight. Some Rotarians visited Moldova and wanted to send shoeboxes for Christmas to Moldova as they had done for many years to Romania. However, as they collected the shoeboxes, they came to realize that Moldova is outside the EU, and that crossing the border is different from going to Romania.

The first thing they did was to contact the Moldovan Embassy in London, as I had at the beginning. This time the Embassy did things in a better way. They gave the Rotary Club members a list of documents needed in Romanian and on the bottom, added my email address and contact number, thinking that, as they were from Isle of Wight, I could help. This was Christmas 2013, precisely when we were beginning to make a difference. I translated the document and helped to complete the paperwork and am happy to report that, years later, Rotary shoeboxes are still going to Moldova.

We are deeply indebted to Rotary Clubs for their assistance in our work, especially the Shanklin Rotary and Ryde Rotary.

Recently we have set new partnership with Dent Aid, an organization with over twenty years experience bringing dental equipment into the most remote areas, and teaching the importance of dental hygiene in schools across the globe. In 2017 they began working in Moldova, installing dental surgery equipment in ten schools, bringing volunteers, and supporting the centers as well.

For me personally—and we try to make this our charity message as well—I've learned that only by working together can we accomplish great results. I have not found a charity that is working for itself; every single one of them is working for their beneficiaries: children, elderly people, those who are ill, abused and so on. But, for some reason, many of these same charities are fearful or reluctant to work together. I never understood why, but I hope that MAD-Aid—together with our friends and supporters across the globe, in the U.K., the States, Switzerland, Ireland and other countries—has established a template for mutual cooperation that will serve as a model not only in Moldova, but all countries that are struggling to lift themselves out of poverty and into the realm of contributing members of the world community.

Part Two

The Big Dream

Chapter Eight

'Salvia'

In 1987, in my hometown of Mihaileni, a stream of therapeutic mineral water was discovered at a depth of 600 meters. Shortly thereafter, the town developed the property on which it was located as a spa call Salvia, which quickly became popular throughout the Soviet Union as a rehabilitation centre. My mother used to work there as nurse and I often went with her to work or to attend different events. For me, it was a place of happy memories and it grew very close to my heart. I treasure those memories still.

At that time, with a staff of over seventy, it was the largest employer in the community.

However, by the time I was eyeing it as a possible site for the daycare centre for disabled children that I envisioned, Salvia had been closed for fourteen years. This was due to the fact that, after the last treatment was given, it closed ostensibly for three months during the winter period because the community couldn't afford to heat it.

Sadly, it never opened again.

It had been such a wonderful setting, newly furnished throughout, a lovely design, all sorts of equipment—and it was simply locked. No one had the initiative, the leadership, or the determination to take whatever steps were necessary to reopen it. No one took responsibility for restoring employment to the seventy people who had lost their jobs.

It was the classic example of Moldovan reaction to opportunity: look for the difficulties, get discouraged, and give up.

Within a few years, it was home to the local vermin. Slowly, like many other institutions and organizations that had ceased operating, it was broken into, stripped of its contents, and destroyed. What had been the thriving, pulsing heart of the community—a Moldovan treasure—stood forgotten, distorted, and wasted by time, neglect, and incompetent management in the 1990s.

For me, it was a crime to let it close, to let it be destroyed like this. The more I thought about it, the more determined I became to reopen it, first as a centre for disabled children; then, who knew? We might coax the whole complex back to life, and bring new light back to the village, my village. Our trustees agreed.

Knowing that the buildings were buried in weeds and, in effect, disintegrating, I was confident that as soon as I asked for it in order to do something for the good of the community, everyone would jump at the opportunity. I told everyone about my plans for Salvia! After all, it was a win-win proposition. Who could possibly object?

What we hadn't taken into account was the stubborn, simple-minded obduracy of Moldovan bureaucrats.

What I hadn't been aware of, as my plans were forming, was that Salvia was no longer owned by the village, but, owing to some obscure documentary gap, had been taken over by the Horticulture Union Department.

Me being me, I began knocking on doors, and if I couldn't find a door, I'd pry open a window! My research led me to the responsible person, and we agreed to meet. Bear in mind I was living in the U.K., working full time, so everything would have to be accomplished during a one-to-two week trip while on holiday in Moldova.

I scheduled the meeting and arrived fully expecting that these people, who, after all, owned Salvia, would know something about it, and would appreciate the beauty of its surroundings and its potential as did I. With my eyes closed, I could recall to memory every nook and cranny.

Imagine my surprise upon hearing the people from the union speak through Serghei, their chief spokesman, that they'd never seen the place! They knew nothing of the decrepit state of the building that was falling further into ruin every day, and it seemed they couldn't care less. To them, Salvia was a deed and a mound of moldy paperwork. Not even a building, but an object, an 'asset' somewhere in the north.

When I presented my idea for a possible collaboration and partnership, the immediate answer was, 'We can't give it to you for free!' Instead, they suggested we buy it for about 200,000 euros!

My counter suggestion—that they give us at least five years rent-free which would allow us time to refurbish it— was met with suspicion. They wanted to know what I was getting out of it. And, furthermore intimated the inevitable question, what would *they* get out of it?

I was appalled and heartbroken.

This was my first taste of the shocking reality of Moldovan corruption. This was more than just a slap in the face; it was a lack of concern for disabled children that, to me, bordered on the depraved. Nevertheless, I pressed on and the conversation opened up to other options, during which they casually mentioned that other people were interested in the property. Had this been the case, of course, the mayor would have known and told me. I think they expected to prompt me to make an offer and were, therefore, surprised when I said that was fine by me. What I wanted, more than anything, was to see Salvia refurbished and working for the village.

Seeing that their pressure tactic had not worked, they suggested that they would draft me an 'anti-contract'. This, even I knew, was not a term that exists in the Moldovan law. Not even in English law is there such a term as 'anti-contract'. Either you get a draft contract, or a temporary contract, or a binding contract. The document they offered stated only that if I could prove that MAD-Aid had sufficient funds to cover the rent for a year, they would offer me a few months free rent.

For us this was not an option, not least because there was no functional structure left at the site for us to pay rent on! The building was dilapidated, with no electricity, no heating, or water, no sewage, no windows, and a leaking roof!

I took the so-called 'anti-contract' and drove back to the village, angry, upset, and with so many mixed feelings. How, I wondered, could Serghei and his cronies sleep at night? Was it something I had done? Had he not taken me seriously? Or was he just another bureaucratic parasite on society? Arriving in the village about 7 pm, I went directly to the mayor's office and told him the details of the meeting.

As you can imagine, the mayor, who wants infrastructure in the village, who wants jobs and who knows how badly this gem of a building is being wasted, was devastated and upset; even more than me, I think. He promised to try and bring the building back to the village. He found the lacunas omissions in the paperwork and discovered how the building had essentially been 'legally' stolen. So he held a village meeting asked people to sign a petition and tried very hard to bring Salvia back into the ownership of the village. I still had high hopes for Salvia, and I didn't look for another building for a while, even though we felt we were a long way from any significant progress.

Fast forward a few years. Salvia is finally, once again, under the ownership of the village, but by that time we were already half way through building Phoenix Centre, our daycare and medical facility for disabled children, in Rîşcani. Today, because of bureaucratic shortsightedness, greed, and corruption, Salvia remains empty and is quickly becoming a ruin. My heart goes out to the many people from the village who contact me and implore me each time I visit, to reclaim the building before it is gone beyond hope.

Chapter Nine

The Phoenix Centre: Beginning Again

While waiting for Salvia to become available, we were continuing to make a difference by delivering aid. And after that event in Bălți when I witnessed so much potential in those children with disabilities, when I witnessed the mistake of calling them bed-bound, when I understood that actually a wheelchair does not make much difference, I realized we needed this centre sooner rather than later. I wanted to make it happen as soon as possible. Those who know me will know that 'soon' means 'yesterday'.

So we started looking for alternative buildings, and in the end, decided to work with the Mayor of Rîșcani, Victor Bogatico, who showed us a few options and who understood that he had to do everything in his power not to let us go.

In Moldova there are many abandoned buildings that closed during the dissolution of the Soviet Union. Some of them have been looked after better than others. Some have just been left alone among the weeds and fall further into ruin by the day. Victor showed us about half a dozen of them. By this time I didn't want to pay any rent at all, just as I was thinking for Salvia.

The mayor understood the importance of this project for the city and its people. However, his board wasn't as reasonable. The memory is painfully fresh. I stood in front of the board, about fifty people, giving a PowerPoint presentation about what MAD-Aid had already done and what we planned to do, and at the end, the very first questions was: 'What are we getting out of this?' By 'we', they meant not the community they served, but they themselves. It took considerable effort, but I politely explained that they would get jobs, that isolated children would have somewhere to go, the city would get the investment, no matter how big or small it is. Nevertheless, the question kept arising in different forms from different members.

By the end of the meeting I lost my temper and my answer was pretty direct and probably didn't sound as polite: 'Does anyone know what *I* am getting out of this?' The room went quiet. 'Nothing! All I want is to change few lives. To help children in *your* district!' Still, their mindsets are so Soviet that, even today, they suspect I must be getting lots of money out of it, otherwise I wouldn't be doing it.

Abandoned elementary school in Rîşcani. 'Why are you doing this?'

I'm about to launch on a little diatribe, so if diatribes offend you, you may wish to skip the next couple of paragraphs. I would be less than honest, however, if I omitted my feelings of frustration and, thereby, left my readers with the impression that this kind of calcified thinking is easily overcome.

I long to live in a world where people can just do good without having their motives questioned, where it is understood that the reward is in the doing: in the smile on a person's face when they are empowered to rise above their disability, whatever it is. If *that* is your expectation, you will never be disappointed. If self-enrichment is your goal, as it was for the people on that board, at that time, you will never be fulfilled.

They represent a type, though, that seems to predominate in bureaucracies: the type who are first in line for a handout, and last to offer a hand up. At the individual level, they are the first to complain of personal hardships, and to blame them on the government, the church, their neighbor, fate, and last to take any personal responsibility. Collectively, they are obstructionists, who expend tremendous amounts of time and energy to interfere with progress, of which they are pathologically suspicious. They are masters of inertia, who don't consider a day well spent unless it has produced several hundred pages of useless regulations.

The good thing is that, though they think themselves untouchable, their ideas *can* be shifted, and I proved it in many cases.

That's the end of the diatribe. Thanks for your patience. I feel much better!

Anyway, the meeting finished and I was still not sure whether or not we were getting the building. By this point I was vacillating between going to Chişinău and demanding of the government why we were getting so much resistance, and just giving up.

Oh, yes! I was tempted to give up on an almost daily basis, and I often felt I didn't have the strength to carry on. It was a temptation I'm simply too obstinate to yield to. I was determined to push on to demonstrate, if nothing else, that it was possible. I refused to accept as fact—like everyone else seemed to do—that everyone in the Moldovan bureaucracy was corrupt, and that it was pointless to fight them. That kind of thinking is an excuse not to try.

If I gave up—if everyone gave up—the children I hoped to serve would have no future. They and thousands like them might just as well be buried now. It was thinking of them that, on many occasions, was all that kept me going; I had looked into their eyes. No, that's not right. I had looked *beyond* their eyes, beyond their disability into their humanity, their long-suffering, and the dignity with which they faced a life in which so many indignities were heaped upon them.

Anyway, at long last the meeting concluded with an agreement for a forty-nine year lease on a Soviet-era kindergarten—a massive concrete hulk on the edge of town that had been abandoned for nearly twenty years. The contract was signed and sealed. The building was spacious, and in need of lots of work, but it's a universal truth that visionaries have eye problems: they don't see what *is*, they see what *will be*. And what I saw as John and I wandered the windowless halls, picking our way through piles of debris and decay, was beautiful.

Passing the meeting with the local authorities was just one of the hurdles. Now I had to persuade my trustees that we could do it. I was dreading that trustee meeting. My stomach was in knots as I entered the room and saw everyone seated there with their copy of the contract that had been drafted by a Moldovan solicitor. Such contracts are very standardized in Moldova, but I had asked for one to be specially done with an eye toward this presentation, and I suspected it was quite poor compared to British rental agreements.

However, after discussing all the possibilities and pitfalls, I was given the okay to sign the contract on behalf of MAD-Aid. I don't want to leave the impression that this concession was given enthusiastically. I don't recall anyone jumping up and down or giving one another high-fives. In truth, they were all pretty worried. Fact is, though I tried to look brave and confident, inside I was more concerned than the rest of them put together. I was conscious that just wanting something, no matter how much, is not going to be enough to accomplish it. MAD-Aid was not set up as charity with millionaire patrons behind the scenes, or with the backing of deep-pocketed founders. We were a small charity, relying on random donations, a few special events, and a handful of volunteers raising funds.

The trustees took modest comfort in a clause in the contract that allowed us three years to start the work, otherwise the building would simply be repossessed. Psychologically, that worked to my advantage in obtaining their approval. They knew there was an escape clause if things didn't work out; no harm, no foul.

That evening when I knew that now it was all down to me, I lay in bed happy, both happy and anxious: happy that I was one step closer to making my dream a reality, but anxious about what lay ahead. What next? How was I to move forward?

I had the building. Great. I also had, in effect, two sets of masters—the trustees on one hand and the people in Moldova on the other—who would be watching my every move, both asking the same questions: 'What, exactly, is it going to be? When will construction begin? Who will work there? How will you train them? Where will you find the children you hope the centre will serve?' And, in the case of our new neighbors: 'Can you give me (or my son, daughter, brother, sister, son-in-law, daughter-in-law, cousin, cousin's daughter's mother's best friend's niece) a job?' Many of these questions were rhetorical. There was no immediate answer. How could I tell someone if I would be able to employ them when I wasn't yet sure what skill sets we would need?

In fact, I didn't even have a full-time job myself!

Nevertheless, John and I went back to Rîșcani and signed the contract, giving local authorities three months to remove all the useless old furniture that was still inside. As we walked around the building, we looked in silence at one another, thinking, 'This is a mess, but now it's ours'. I had the key, and I could come and go as I pleased.

MAD-Aid was the proud owner of a place to build a dream.

Whenever I'm in Moldova, I try to meet as many people as possible to create partnerships, to maybe learn something new or lay the foundation for some funding later. Early on, very few took me seriously. Who was I but a silly girl who didn't know what is she talking about; just another dreamer whose dreams would die on the vine? Even though, to some, I had proved myself by delivering tonnes of aid and successfully passing the customs clearance hurdle—against all odds and with no bribe—most were unconvinced and refused to take me seriously.

During the contract-signing trip, I also thought to try and go to the Minister of Social Protection to ask if I needed any permission in order to open the centre, and if there was anything I needed to be aware of. This was yet was another bad and disappointing meeting. The vice minister of Social Protection told me—between the lines—that children with disabilities are not worth the investment, because, in his words, 'It's not as though you will be able to do anything for them, or give them any future.'

In another famous phrase, the minister told me, 'You are young and you don't know anything about how to run a centre. I studied management in the Soviet Union at Moscow University and I know that it is very difficult'. I recall this phrase many times with a smile: the famous statement of many. Soviet Union people, I call them.

I couldn't understand why this man couldn't think, for five minutes of the people he was supposed to be serving. He said the 200,000 Euros I estimated the centre would cost was 'not a significant sum of investment.' Maybe not to him! I was amazed that he seemed unable to realize that an investment, however modest, is still an investment, and it will still provide a few jobs and will still bring added value into the local community.

I began to weep, not for myself but because I had come to the Minister of Labour, Social Protection and the Family— the very person who should be the most powerful and persuasive advocate for people struggling with disabilities— and he simply didn't want to know.

I thought, if I come *with* help and am treated like this, what was happening to people who came to him *for* help?! My tears were flowing at the understatement that the country is so messed up, with two or three different types of world in one square kilometer, no human rights, no disabled people on the map, no worries about those who need help, or those who want to help.

At this point I started crying openly. John was with me, of course, and though he didn't understand what we were talking about, he saw my tears. As if it weren't enough that the minister had interrupted our twenty-minute meeting five times to take phone calls—a rudeness John could barely tolerate—seeing me cry nearly sent him over the edge. 'Please translate for me or I'm going to deck this bloke. I don't care who he is…'

I was confused and upset, but pulled myself together, and determined not to let the minister get under my skin. He will remain in my memory as an uncaring and dreadful man. That is a sad legacy. It may not even be an accurate impression of him. Maybe he was having a bad day. Maybe someone had run over his dog. I don't know. What I do know is that I came to him for advice, a simple walk-through process, or even the name of someone else I could contact. And he didn't take me seriously. In the few minutes he had to give me his full attention, he accused me of not coming with a business plan and proposal. I took it out of my case and dropped it on his desk. He looked at it disdainfully and said it was not his job to look through it.

He didn't even care that John, a foreigner who had just spent one year raising funds and collecting aid to help Moldova's disadvantaged, was in the room. For all the minister knew, John might have been a major donor, who would not have been impressed with this treatment. Did the minister with his Soviet mentality care? Not in the least.

I realized now that, just as I was learning everything in U.K. about how to start and run a charity and to fundraise, so I would learn in Moldova how to start, run and open a centre. More closed doors lay ahead—doors that had never been opened before, whose hinges were rusted shut—and we would simply have to knock them down.

By now my vision was fully developed on paper. We had the backing of the mayor of Rîşcani. We had the building. We had storage spaces overflowing with donated furniture and equipment, but that was no good unless we repaired and refurbished the building, and for that, we needed money.

That meant a miracle.

This, I think, is what happened with our long-standing partnership between MAD-Aid and the Communications Workers Union Humanitarian Aid organization, CWUHA.

During CWUHA's Annual General Meeting, when, you remember, I was asked to give a talk, John had mentioned our aim of opening a centre for children with disabilities and suggested their returning to Moldova for their 20th anniversary year. Almost off-handedly, we suggested, 'Why don't you help us to refurbish the children's part of the centre as your 20th year project? Build something lasting that will bring smiles to the faces of needy children, not just twice a year, but every day.'

Unexpectedly, I got a call from Carl Webb, chair of CWUHA, inviting me to a meeting in London to present the project in more detail. It is very easy for me to talk about MAD-Aid and Moldova Aid. They're my brainchildren, and their story is written on my heart. So, of course, I jumped at the chance to tell it.

As a result of that meeting, CWUHA sent two of its trustees to Moldova and we inspected the building together. I also gave them a copy of the structural report. The building was really strong; even the few outbuildings outside were extremely strong. (We decided later to demolish two of them and broke two JCB tractors in the demolition process!) So, the structural report was not an issue at all.

When an irresistible force meets an immovable object!

After that visit, I was invited to Manchester for a trustee's meeting. Great. Another meeting. As I entered the room, I couldn't shake my memory of that earlier meeting with the Minister of Social Protection in Moldova. Mentally, I prepared for the worse. The project was scrutinized, and questioned by all the members. But these were different sorts of questions. They seemed aimed at trying to find ways in which CWUHA could help, rather than ridiculing the project or throwing obstacles in its way. I was encouraged. Still, in charity projects, you can never know which way the wind is blowing. Will they partner with you? Do they actually have the funds? Will they really give them to you? Sometimes, at the last minute, plans laid with the best of intentions will simply fall through, for one reason or another. You never really know until you have the contract and the money's in the bank.

At the conclusion of the meeting, we got the go-ahead! MAD-Aid had a not only won a powerful new partner, but a raft of faithful new friends who have stood with us shoulder-to-shoulder throughout the transformation process.

So, in November 2014, funding in the amount of £40,000 was agreed to refurbish phase one: a daycare for disabled children, with plans to open during the visit of the September 2015 Convoy. That gave us nine months to raise from the remains of a derelict Soviet kindergarten a modern centre built on the British model. And I was still working 40+ hours in NHS!

Phoenix bold and fiery logo by Andy Buchanan

Furthermore, CWUHA agreed to bring furniture and equipment for the centre in their May and September convoys. In recognition of all their efforts on the centre's behalf, we offered CWUHA the opportunity to name it. Eventually I was informed that they would like it to be called the Phoenix Centre! Perfect!

As time passed, the project seemed to get bigger and bigger. We were a small charity with five non-paid members in the U.K. and a few inexperienced volunteers in Moldova. Often, too often, I'd get scared and find myself plagued by doubt; this was growing out of hand. Could I really pull this off? I felt so helpless. Then I would close my eyes and call to mind Alexandru and the look on his face as he received our very first wheelchair. I'd hear the words of Igor, who, taking possession of his chair, said that his only dream was 'a world without stairs'.

Over the years, I've learned the art of hiding my fears: I just shove them aside and plow ahead, even if I'm not exactly sure what comes next. I focus on the big picture and imagine how great this complex will be when it becomes self-supporting, how many children and young people we will help become functional, and in many cases self-reliant, members of society. That focus gives me strength and helps me silence those fears.

Chapter Ten

Live and Learn

I had the project, I had the budget, I had a clear picture what I wanted, but there was still not enough money, and, being new to fund-raising, had no idea where it would come from. But I was reminded of what Nelson Mandela said when confronted with the enormity of the task before him: 'A thing is only impossible until it is done'.

Once again I was at the beginning—another beginning, but still a beginning. I knew what I wanted to do, and what I needed to do it. Now I had to learn how to go about getting it done!

The trustees, very wisely, told me to start by writing it all down. It's surprising how my plans began to acquire structure when I put them down in black and white. I'm so fortunate to have such a great board of trustees to help put flesh on the bones of my ideas. Ever since then, before talking about my ideas, I write them down, so they are clear and orderly in my mind. Otherwise, how can I hope to communicate them in a way that is comprehensible to my hearers?

So, I had taken a big step. There were my plans. I could put them in anyone's hands. Anyone could read them. But still, they were only plans. The question now was, how would I fulfill them?

I've come to believe that, somewhere, there's a book someone's written that has the solution to just about any practical problem. Perhaps if you had enough time to read all the books and the power to put their principles into action, most of the world's problems could be solved.

My problems, however, were not the world's problems. I just needed those two or three books that would teach me how to solve those I faced.

Fortunately, I love reading. I downloaded to my Kindle many books: fundraising, project management, time management. That doesn't mean I became an expert in each field as I read, but I was able to glean a great deal of useful information, much of which was so obvious I'd overlooked it completely, but was powerful when put into practice.

The same goes for fundraising. There needs to be constant forward momentum, constant learning and trying different approaches, different audiences, talking to many people and, for the sake of one's sanity, laying down expectations. It took me a long time to learn not to expect anything. Phoenix is desperately important to me. I've looked into the eyes of the people it will serve; I know their stories, but someone else may be just as passionate about another charity, and that is, understandably, where their allegiance lies, toward which they will direct their efforts, and for which they will open their pocket books.

Learning to respect people's choices and responses—even their silence—took me long time, especially on those occasions when, moved by emotion of the moment, they made promises they didn't keep.

Now I come out of meetings with an open mind, and when asked how it went, my response is simply 'We'll see'!

There are some subjects, though, that no amount of reading or instruction seems to have an effect on. My particular struggle is time management—even after years of effort. Very rarely do I include time for John, for our family, or even for myself. And, on those rare occasions when I do, I feel guilty for not working! As if eight to five is not enough, I labour on until 10 or 11 in my home office, crawl into bed, kiss John goodnight—though he's most often asleep by that time—and virtually expire until the first light of day filters through our window.

That's not healthy. Not for me. Not for my marriage; Ultimately, not for MAD-Aid, either. Because if I drive myself to exhaustion—or to an early grave—what good will I be to anyone?

Any psychologist will tell you that the first step toward solving a problem is admitting you have one. 'Only by naming a beast, can you slay it,' someone once said. Well, I know my beast: its name is Time Management, and I'm determined to bring it to heel. I have to say that reading *7 Habits of Highly Influential People* has given me perspective, and I'm beginning to get a handle on this problem.

Phoenix Rising!

With first payment from CWUHA in the bank, it was time to start. The Moldova AID team was employed: three full-time and one part-time staff, plus three night watchmen; and because the roof and windows needed to be repaired or replaced before we could set about the rest of the work, they were instructed to look for a roof and window contractor.

And here's where the real fun began. All the locals were under the impression that, since the money came from the U.K., there was no end of it, and that we wouldn't mind what they charged. This was far from reality. Yes, the money came from the U.K., but every penny was strictly budgeted and I would have to give an account of it to the trustees!

Every step of the way I negotiated to get the best possible deal. The charity may be British, but I am still Moldovan, so it is very hard to get some bureaucratic nonsense past me.

Which is not to say I didn't have to put up with it. Here are a few examples: The phone rings. It's 6:00 in the morning,

U.K. time, which means 8:00 a.m. in Moldova. My brother Oleg is on the line:

'The electrician is going to Chişinău today. He wants 30,000 leis so he can buy electric cable for the centre'. Bear in mind this was an early morning call and, as John will attest, I'm not at my most agreeable early in the morning. Furthermore, I haven't seen the quotes for the electrical work. And, even if I had, how could I be expected, on short notice, and without a contract, to transfer 30,000 MDL (£1200) to Moldova! On top of that, I had made it abundantly clear that I personally had to negotiate every single purchase, even if it would only save £10, I still tried my best.

'We need to clean the grounds. Do we buy some tools or should we borrow them?' was another question early one morning. When I asked how much the tools would be, it was about 60-100 MDL (less than £5).

I realized that I needed to introduce some basic ground rules about how much my staff could spend without prior authorization. And I had to teach them how to deal with the project finance. All of which meant that I had to learn to be a better project manager. I'm still learning this constantly from books, webinars, as well as from experience—and six a.m. wake up calls!

Challenges like this also made me realize that I needed to broaden my skill set if were to pull off this project successfully. My most immediate task was to go to Moldova and sort out the contractors.

Accordingly, in March 2015, I went to Rîşcani and, with help of the local team and a carefully review of references, identified the outdoor contractors—those who would work on the roof, the outside walls, and the grounds—and the indoor contractors, who would take care of everything other than electricity and heating.

The window contractor negotiated with shops for materials, but had a hard time because merchants were so skeptical about the viability of the project. Very few people could see the importance of it, *very few*! And none wanted to be part of it.

I had to accept this attitude as a fact of life, at least until we proved them wrong.

My constant problem was budget and time, and both of them were very short supply. I had to study each quote to identify what materials could be obtained cheaper and from where. For example if electrical cable was cheaper in the U.K., we'd buy it there; if something was cheaper in Moldova, we would buy it there. And, in the back of my mind, I was cognizant of the fact that every purchase diminished our bank account proportionately, so I was constantly trying to raise more funds—or at least thinking about ways in which to do so.

Addressing these problems and challenges so occupied my time that it soon became impossible for me to do my normal night shifts, because I had no time to rest. There were stretches of time when I went 48 hours without sleep. Slowly I became increasingly reliant on John's income. He didn't mind, bless him, but being so independent by nature, it was a struggle for me. I still tried to juggle my job, the project, and my home life as much as possible with varying degrees of success.

Each evening, my brother, who was and is the site manager, would send me pictures from the centre of the progress and it looked as though nothing was happening yet. The building was just a shell. I was fully involved and knew pretty much how many screws were needed for a plasterboard panel and how many meters of cable were needed for a room. Sad, I know, but I was overwhelmed by the realization of how big a responsibility I had taken on, and that I had to answer not only to my trustees—who are a very forgiving and encouraging bunch—but to the CWUHA trustees who had entrusted me with so much.

Does the term 'micro-management' come to mind?

All the while, as we collected furniture, equipment, and supplies of various kinds, I was keeping a lookout for a minibus for Phoenix, one that was specially adapted to the needs of children in wheelchairs. Good news; John found one! Bad news; we had to raise the funds to buy it within 24 hours …

In May 2015, John and I drove that minibus from the U.K. to Moldova.

Arriving at the centre, we could already see a real difference. The windows had been installed, everyone was busy working, and we saw some life slowly returning to the forgotten, abandoned building we had left.

But it was still a shell, and that's what the CWUHA team saw when they arrived with the spring convoy, and what Phil Batson, the British Ambassador, saw when he visited the site.

Each night, my brother Oleg sent me pictures of the day's 'progress'

I felt they looked at me with such pity, thinking that I was overly optimistic to imagine the job would be completed by September.

Bear in mind the opening date was set, at CWUHA's request, to coincide with the arrival of their fall convoy and some of our British invitees already had their flights booked, or had, at least, scheduled their time off work. Personally, I didn't allow myself time to consider the possibility that it wouldn't be done on schedule. I just got on with it.

As I did this, I was determined to make every penny count, to spend it responsibly and to make sure that that on which it was spent met expectations. I was determined not to yield to the conventional Soviet-era way of thinking, which is always with an eye toward wringing benefits for the builders and the authorities, but to make everyone consider, first and foremost—in tasks large and small—the benefit to the children, the community, and the future.

One of these considerations, which was non-negotiable, was accessibility. From the start, we were aware that it was not going to be easy to adapt a Soviet-era building, which had virtually no amenities for the disabled, to one that would meet EU standards in that regard, but I was sure it could be done, and said so. We asked the architect and the building inspector for the site to come and give us advice about building an access ramp. Here is the advice we were given:

'Just put it on the existing stairs.' This is the common solution in Moldova. It is simple, cheap, and gives the appearance, at least, of having made some accommodation for people with disabilities. In fact, all you have in the end is a deadly slide at a 45-degree gradient that, were he wheelchair-bound, would give Superman a hernia!

The second solution: 'It's impossible!' (Another familiar Moldovan refrain) 'Leave as it is and make the ramp at the back!' This underscored the fact that the speaker hadn't gotten his head around the concept that this centre was entirely for disabled children, and their needs were of primary concern, not those of guests, staff, or anyone else.

'To do it the way you want is simply going to be too expensive.' Well, they were right about that!

We responded to all these silly ideas, especially the first one, with real attitude. Why were people so blind to the needs of wheelchair-users. John went to a storeroom in Rîșcani where we kept two foldable ramps to be used when we were taking the children out and about, as very few places were accessible. This he unfolded on the first three steps and proceeded to offer a wheelchair to the inspector to have a go. He declined. (Imagine that!) But one of the workers tried. Though the ramp covered only three steps, it impossibly steep, and the trial was a failure.

Three steps! What would happen when it had to cover ten steps? Fifteen? Twenty?!

Mumbling something about my being too young, and a girl, and not grasping the complexities or the job, the building inspector decided he didn't want to work with me anymore. John responded by telling me to remove him from the site, and not allow him back. 'Fly in the treacle, that bloke,' he said. I'm not familiar with the saying, but I think I got the idea.

I haven't seen that individual since.

Which is not to say I don't need help. I never pretended that I knew everything. That's why I always seek the help and advice of people who do, or should know. But sometimes you have to take that advice for what it's worth. For instance, when the owner of a construction company invited John and me to see the beautiful ramp he had built in the Courtroom, we loaded a wheelchair in the boot of the car and off we went.

The builder was absolutely right, the ramp was beautifully done, cosmetically, and will very likely stay new-looking forever, because it is impossible to use! The angle is probably 45 degrees, not the maximum 6 as permitted by EU standards, and it's covered in shiny tiles that are slippery in rain, fog, or snow—for all of which Rîşcani is noted. Even the width between the rails is not standard!

That's not a ramp. It's a sculpture.

Eventually we found *real* architect—that is, one whose job was finding solutions, not bowing to challenges—and he did the plans. The resulting ramp is thirty-seven meters long, and it was even more expensive than anticipated, but it's there. It works. It meets EU standards. And, most important of all, it makes the centre accessible for the disabled children to whom it is home away from home.

Innately, I'm a trusting person, and not suspicious. Unfortunately, that attitude had to change. I had to come to grips with the fact that those hired to work on the project were there for the money. Few had any concern for the children. It is tragic to think about, but I had to be very careful tracking inventory so as not to get ripped off, or have precious equipment and materials stolen. For example, my brother Oleg, the site manager, would have to count the number of sacks of cement left on the site, every evening, to make sure that none went walk-about.

This side of project was very upsetting and it still is now when someone tries to take advantage. I wonder how people can sleep at night if they try to rip off projects like this. It is not as though we were making money or trying to do business—not that that would be any excuse—but we were only trying to help those who couldn't help themselves. All we wanted was to have our work, our time, and our intentions respected.

I had heard rumors of foreign investors and companies who had come to Moldova hoping to open factories, start businesses, provide jobs (and pay taxes!) only to leave in disgust when confronted by a wall of corruption, short-sightedness, ignorance, and greed at every turn. I saw it now first-hand. I thought, how could a foreigner make a go of it in Moldova when there was no way of knowing whom to trust?

I realized, too, that the blame for the endemic problems in Moldova wasn't entirely attributable to the government. To a great extent, the people themselves, by their own actions, or inaction, and attitude, invite poverty. It is this, together with government dysfunction that is manifested in the condition of the country as a whole. Everyone professes to want change, but very few are willing to begin that change within themselves.

The challenges continued. The companies with which we contracted for work had tacit, unwritten non-compete agreements with competitors, effectively establishing monopolies relative to a particular job. Which meant lack of competition. Which meant inflated prices and reduced quality work. This is especially so with infrastructure, such as gas, Internet, phone, electricity. As an example, when an electrician from Rîşcani showed me the quote for part one of the project—installing the cabling—my response was to ask for the quote for part two, which was adding the sockets and light switches so I could determine their affordability. As part one was very expensive, I thought if part two is just as expensive, we've got a struggle on our hands.

Next day I received a quote for part two, and it seemed really cheap. We could just swing the combined figures.

Of course, I'd tried to get other companies to quote, but everyone refused as soon as they found out who gave us the first quote, arguing that they did not want to tread on each other's toes. So, we contracted the Rîșcani company with their assurance that they had given me a discount.

Fortunately, when they began the job, John was there to oversee their work. Again and again he made them go back and redo what they had done. My position as translator—when I didn't know how things should be done—proved to be extremely difficult. I knew that I wanted the centre wired as in the U.K., thirteen-amp ring mains with British sockets on the walls, but the engineering of it was alien to me. John would get upset thinking that I was not listening to him, and the electrician would look at me as if I was stupid. All I was doing was translating!

Anyway, we got to part two, and new costs came to light. Apparently, when I was given the original quote for part two, it was only as an example for one room. This nearly put an end to the project. When I thought the electrical work was all sorted, we had to find another huge sum, about £2500. We were in the middle of the project, and we even tried to get electricians from Chișinău and the other side of the country, but none would take on the job halfway through. They told me it would be a sure-fire way to kill yourself, as you would not know what was done during the first part of the installation.

Finally, I managed to have an advocate in the government apply a little pressure and we managed get about

£1000 knocked off the cost. That about wiped us out, but we went ahead.

As you can imagine, the experience left me feeling pretty upset.

Having the electric system installed is one thing. Arranging for the supply of electricity is another. Only one company, Red Nord, supplies the north of Moldova. They had to sign off the work and set up a monthly-paid supply contract with us. The local management team normally deals with such things, but I happened to be driving on the occasion when the director, Mariana Botnari, went to Red Nord to set up the supply contract.

The Red Nord Customer Service Officer explained the monthly supply rate, and that we had to take out separate contracts for the three electricity distribution poles that carried the power from the supply station to the centre. I burst laughing automatically, uncontrollably.

'WHAT? We have to pay rent for the poles supplying the electricity that we pay you for?'

'Yes,' he replied calmly, 'those are the rules for organizations, for non-residential users.' The amount is negligible, 200 MDL per year—less than £10—so not worth the paper the contract is printed on. It's the fact that there have to be separate contracts that's ridiculous. Somewhere, I'm convinced, tucked away in some dingy little office, is a government employee whose job it is to create ways to generate more paper work. They're probably taking bribes from the paper companies! So, here we were, having to take time filling out more unnecessary paperwork. I couldn't help but think it was like pulling into petrol station for a fill up, and being told you have to pay twice, once for the gas, and once for the hose, and you have to fill out forms for both!

The fee for the poles could simply and easily have been included in the price of the electricity. I found this amusing and funny, probably in the wrong way. He suggested that if I didn't want to pay, I could put up my own poles.

Yes, I thought, I'll get right on that.

Why? Why, I wondered, does Moldova make itself look so stupid and primitive to the world?

It was exactly the same when it came to installing the heating. Originally a company quoted over 400,000 MDL. I said this was an awful lot more than even I expected, and asked whether it included all the necessary planning permissions and everything else. They confirmed that it did. Still, I refused the quotation. It was simply too expensive. We managed to get someone to install the central heating system much more cheaply with the understanding that all I would have to do would be to purchase the heating boilers and have gas brought to the building.

Easy? This is Moldova.

We brought the gas to the building, and I thought it would be as simple as buying a Vaillant boiler and connecting A to B.

Not so fast!

Because the company with which we had contracted was allowed to install only one type of gas boiler, made by Termona—of which there is only one supplier in the whole country—and there had to be two of these in case one broke down, to which must be added all sort of pumps and automatic controls, the cost of connecting A to B would run to a further £15000 pounds.

John almost exploded! I nearly fainted.

So at the last minute, we decided to install a biomass (green energy) boiler, and this is what we are using now. But getting there was a long journey on a slow train, punctuated by many sleepless nights.

All this is made even more sad when looked at from a business perspective. I don't understand how these people think! I still have three blocks to be refurbished and would gladly have worked with them again had they been competent, reasonable, and honest. Now, of course, that won't happen, even if I have to bring electricians and plumbers from the U.K.

I still sometimes blame myself for my naïveté, and not recognizing how cheap and underhanded some people can be. Many people took advantage of me and, in so doing, they were taking advantage of the children the centre now serves. At the end of the day I believe everyone will answer for their behavior in this life, and I wouldn't want to be in their shoes when that time comes. I'm not going to stop changing children's lives just because I was taken advantage of.

Nor am I going to be bitter and cynical, simply 'wise as a serpent, and gentle as a dove,' as Jesus said. As Mum always reminds me, 'Be patient, Vitoria. Not everyone is like you!' I think I must have earned my MAD Woman label long before this project!

The next step was to employ people for the new centre. I knew that CVs were very rarely used in Moldova, especially in the villages, so I created an application form and put copies in the job centre office, in the offices of local authorities, as well as in our office.

Reading through applications and trying to shortlist them was hilarious. One applicant said, 'I want nice conditions and short hours.' And the interviews were even more interesting. At one of them, to the question, 'Why should we hire you, why are you better than others?' the answer was: 'I don't know, I never met the others.'

Fortunately, we had many applications and we managed to select what felt like a good team. Everyone was on a 6-month probation period, at the end of which we only had to replace a few.

The last bombshell over the construction work came from the parliament of Moldova. The project was financed fully by British donations for the benefit of the Moldovan community, in our case, for disabled children. There is a clear clause in Moldovan legislation that exempts foreign organizations investing in construction in Moldova from payment of VAT tax, with Parliamentary approval. At the end of March or the beginning of April, I applied for a certificate of VAT exemption, with every confidence that I would get it as everything had been done strictly by the book.

I had reached agreement with our suppliers and contractors to let us pay the last 20% once we had this letter so that the full invoice would come with no VAT. By July, though, I had no response to my application. When I tried to get an answer, I was stonewalled.

I tried to contact the relevant department and failed.

I asked Phil Batson, the British Ambassador, to help and get involved. He kindly did. He sent letters, set up meetings, and was promised that it was nearly sorted out. The beginning of August came and went without the letter— and Parliament went on holiday for six weeks.

My heart sank. This meant that many more thousands of pounds (around £10,000, if I recall correctly) would have to be found in days. Every hour counted. Opening day was just around the corner. What was I supposed to do? People would be showing up to work, and needed to be paid.

Up until then, I had had my budget worked out so perfectly, and pretty much all in line, and then this.

Once again, though I hated to do so, I turned to CWUHA, as well as to Excel Manufacturing, and they stepped up and helped me when I needed them most, for which I'm forever grateful.

To be sure, I learned another valuable lesson from this: In Moldova, you shouldn't make any assumptions, even if there's legislation in black and white, even if you have assurances, and a handwritten promise that 'The check's in the mail.'

As John often says, 'This isn't Earth. It's Moldova!'

I also learned that if you need help, ask. The worst that can happen is you get a 'No'. But keep asking. Eventually, someone will say 'Yes'.

With all the funny, exasperating, nail-biting, head-spinning ups and downs, with all the hurdles and learning curves, we managed to complete the work by the first week of September.

I could probably count how many full days off I had since March 2015! The project completely took over our lives. And I still don't regret one minute, nor do the people that are involved in it.

Chapter Eleven

Phoenix Centre: the Opening

The summer of 2015 had gone by so fast. It felt like I was in planes more than on land. Every evening when I was in the U.K., I would receive pictures updating me on progress from Phoenix. However, the results were becoming so promising that, day by day, we were waiting for the 19th of September when the centre door would be opened to receive the first children for whom the centre was created—just for them, with them always in mind.

During the last six weeks before the opening, I was in Moldova, overseeing the finishing touches, arranging the convoy and the opening festivities, meeting parents, employing people. The days were long—14 hours, 7 days a week—and still there was not enough time. The problems, including the VAT issue, drained me completely. At one point, I was feeling so tired that I thought I would break down. John sensed this on our nightly Skype calls, so he flew over for one week to support me. During that time, he and James Buchanan, our Peace Corps volunteer, assembled most of furniture. John was always there to give me what I needed, whether to anchor me to reality, or to lift me out of discouragement. Phoenix Centre, MAD-Aid and, therefore, this book would not have been possible without him.

The day came when the CWUHA convoy arrived, and then fifteen trustees and guests flew in for the opening. Many were very skeptical and worried that the centre may not be ready after what they had seen in May, but the new building made everyone proud. We did it! We delivered what we said we would, and the trustees of CWUHA, MAD-Aid and Child AID were all on hand to witness what, together, we had achieved. After their arrival and before the official opening, we had two more days during which the drivers, trustees, and volunteers pitched in to deliver aid to hundreds of families.

As it happens, in Moldova it is customary to invite government officials to events like this. Many times I wonder why. Nevertheless, I was told that if they were to attend, their participation would confer special significance upon the project. In our case, we were to be honoured by the attendance of the Prime Minister, together with other relevant ministers, and of course our all-time number one supporter, HM British Ambassador, Phil Batson.

Opening Day: excitement and chaos

I understood that this was a great honour, but I didn't anticipate the challenges presented by security protocols! We had the Prime Minister's security team in for half a day on the day before opening of the centre. The site is quite large and with delivering aid, preparing for the opening, and a charity ball after the opening, I was running around in ever-more-frantic circles. Wherever I was, all I could hear was someone shouting my name. My phone went flat every hour from being overused. John used to joke and say that I would get a brain tumour from talking on the phone so much.

There are scientific studies about how the human brain switches to a kind of default autopilot mode when the brain is overwhelmed. That's exactly what happened to me. I was like a robot. Thank God, we filmed the opening, because looking back I can recall very little. But I proved that my brain works, and functions relatively well in either mode, at least until *that* battery gets flat, too.

Anyway, in all this madness the day of the opening arrived, and from 6 a.m. we had many, many security guards at the centre for the Prime Minister's protection. About 8 a.m., I arrived at the centre and was told at the gate that I could not drive in. As you may imagine, this didn't go down well with me. Call it hubris or what you will, but I felt it was I who should be deciding who was admitted, not them.

They soon realised that there was no point in arguing with me, and I drove in. However, the pressures and inconvenience caused by the presence of these officials, most of whom had done nothing to help bring the centre into being, but were more than willing to take credit, was casting a negative pall over the proceedings.

The level of security was, in my view, ridiculous. Even the Prime Minister's waiter was there! Every item of food and drink to be served to the Prime Minister had to be tasted by the guards, one of whom had the temerity to tell me that John should change his shorts for trousers because the Prime Minister was coming. This was at about 9 a.m.—two hours from opening—and the temperature was 35 degrees. I said: 'John will change for the actual opening because I want him to, not because you told him to, and there are 32 British people coming, who will dress as they like! This is their project and they can do whatever they want'.

With all the last-minute logistics—note that we had thirty-two British guests, about twenty Romanians, and many important people from Moldova from other diplomatic missions, people who had actually contributed and helped make the centre possible—this blind obeisance to protocol was, as the Brits say, getting right up my nose. I was on the verge of forbidding the Moldovan Prime Minister from coming to the opening because of these men! Of course, they were just doing their jobs, but to my frame of mind at the time, they were overdoing it.

John noticed that I was getting upset and wound up, so he jokingly mentioned that there were so many of them at front gate, but none at back gate. 'If you really want to give them fits, tell them we have a Muslim with us,' he said. (One of our lovely CWUHA convoy drivers was Muslim.) What he didn't realise was that the guards spoke English. Within minutes, the back gate was manned by more guards, and you could see the concern on their faces as they scanned the crowd. Looking back, it was funny, but at that moment it was stressful. I certainly learned more about Moldovan protocol than I cared to know. It's the world we live in, I suppose, but I really thought the whole business bordered on the comic.

The opening itself was emotional and overwhelming. There were tears of joy and relief, and nice speeches, especially from the British Ambassador, who said that to have a vision transformed into reality within four months was remarkable, and that his grandfather in the U.K. was once a postman, and would have been very proud to know that his post office not only delivered letters in Britain, but also delivered hope to where it is most needed in the world.

Of course, the children were there too. They didn't understand what was happening to them, or what the fuss was all about. They were scared, desperately shy, and lost, very lost. There was no childhood in them at all. Do you recall Alexandru, the boy that received our first wheelchair? Well, by pure coincidence, the opening of the Phoenix Centre was on his birthday, a date chosen by CWUHA. Everything happens for a reason in this life, and paths cross at the right time. It was Alexandru who cut the ribbon and, one by one, the children stepped into their new daytime home—a world unlike any they had ever known.

The children ranged in age from five to nineteen. Some of them had never had any sort of social inclusion other than maybe the odd hospital trip. We were not surprised that they felt lost, even with their parents or caregivers beside them.

Phoenix Rises! Open the doors!

The Centre echoed with appreciative voices, and the almost constant hum of discussion and networking. In the end, nearly a hundred guests took part in what was an historic event for this part of Moldova. The first phase of the centre was done. Everyone looked genuinely impressed and astonished.

'It always seems impossible until it is done,' as Nelson Mandela had said, and here was our first proof of it.

By mid-afternoon, I was beyond exhaustion, and the evening charity ball was still ahead, together with the last-minute logistics for that too. There was no time to relax yet, but deep inside, I was tremendously relieved by the knowledge that the main thing was done. Phoenix Centre was open! I thought, with a great sense of accomplishment, of all the obstacles, hurdles, and challenges we had overcome in order to deliver what I promised.

Once again, time would reveal my naïveté. The hard work of assuming responsibility for such a huge project had only just begun.

MAD-Aid was the proud owner of the building, and now we were the proud owners of all the challenges and responsibilities that came with its upkeep, maintenance, management, and useful employment. Assembling and managing the construction team suddenly seemed easy. Having responsibility for providing regular paychecks for twenty employees and meeting the many needs of the children, for whom we had such high hopes, was on another level altogether.

Meeting these responsibilities remains a monthly struggle. Many months I could see no way we could meet wages and expenses. The trustees have been so good and, time and again, stepped up to help me, as did CWUHA and many other sponsors and supporters.

Still, as the end of each month draws near, I spend many sleepless nights. During those times, I intentionally call to mind that Saturday of the opening. Sunday was a day off and Monday was Rîşcani City Day and a bank holiday. On Tuesday, John and I were getting ready to fly back to the U.K., but we wanted to visit the centre first. We arrived at the centre at about 10 a.m., and there were the children on their very first working day! I stepped into the room and, finally, all my strength gave way, and the dam burst. I burst into tears, sobbing uncontrollably and had to leave to keep from upsetting the children.

You have this vision, that seems so far away, then you have a plan but no money at all, then you get the money and you start working day by day to bring this project to life. One day the windows get changed and you see the difference in the building, another day the paint is on the walls, and you feel so much closer, then the carpet goes down, the furniture installed and slowly, slowly—as if from nothing, reality is spun from dreams, and you can see an end in sight.

Suddenly the day comes when none of that matters anymore, not the paint, not the type of furniture you have, none of it. You realize that this is it, this is why it was all was done: for them, for these wonderful children. The children gave the centre colour, life, and purpose in a way that no amount of paint could have ever have given. All the hard work seemed so insignificant in comparison to seeing these faces, still shy, still scared, but with so much hope in their eyes which, for the first time, spoke of hope. A few children had their parents with them as they were afraid to be left alone, not understanding that they were now in a world designed—even down to the toilet—was designed just for them, where they could be independent.

Many of the children had had family members caring for them for up to seventeen years, and were completely dependent upon them. Now, perhaps for the first time, child and caregiver were separated. For some, this was a traumatic transition. This is where the teachers stepped in. They were wonderful, despite the fact that dealing with the disabled was new to them and, as on-the-job training, demanded spur-of-the-moment thinking and the development of new skills.

Everyone had been employed on a six-month trial contract. For the most part, this was because I knew it would take a special kind of person to cope with the challenges of the children and their environment. During this trial period, those who were in for the money, or as interim employment would be winnowed out. Those left would have demonstrated that it was their heart that led them, and love for the children that empowered them to rise to those challenges.

I'm pleased to report that almost all our colleagues came through with flying colours.

I had gone to Moldova in the middle of August, when the centre was still a construction site, and by the time I left on September 20th, children were making it their second home. All that time when I was tired, upset, and emotionally bruised from banging my head against another brick wall, I clung to a single thought: It doesn't matter if I die on 20th of September; I will have left something important behind, something positive: a home full of smiles, love and care.

It was all worth it.

Welcome to your new daytime home!

Chapter Twelve

Making a Difference

M.A.D., Making A Difference, is the name of our charity. The Phoenix Centre was started because we saw the need: we identified the injustice that children with special needs were going through. At the end of the day they are exactly the same as any other child, with the same right to be included, to be educated, to be loved. It is a birthright, not a privilege, that we were trying to deliver. Moldovan society is not educated to accept these children as equal. The parents are left to deal with the problems alone, with no significant support, no advice, and no help. In many cases they, too, become isolated.

So many times I wonder, what is disability? Why does it have to be like this? Why, when they put up public buildings in Moldova, do they not offer one accessible path, not one accessible facility? How can you marginalize the people from such a young age and give them a label that will stick with them forever?

In fact, aren't we all disabled in one way or another?

I can't read or write music, or play an instrument. I'm musically disabled. I'm not a lawyer. I have a legal disability. I don't understand differential calculus or the Fibonacci series. I'm mathematically disabled. I have similar disabilities in many other areas. We all do. Yet no one seems to have any difficulty accommodating these deficiencies.

Why do we, as a society, have such difficulty accommodating physical disabilities? It breaks my heart to think of the human potential that's been lost due to their exclusion. What if some Anne Sullivan had not seen beyond the disabilities of Helen Keller, the deaf-blind political activist and writer, and abandoned her to useless isolation because of them? The thousands of lives that have been positively impacted, the immeasurable potential that has been unlocked through her amazing work would have been unrealized.

Yet this is how children and adults with disabilities have been treated, time out of time. In many countries like Moldova and, I imagine, the rest of the countries of the former Soviet Union, they still are.

The loss is ours.

Among the many odds stacked against Phoenix Centre from the beginning was this stereotype: the prevailing opinion, in government circles as well as among the general population, that these children weren't worth the bother. Phoenix was built, in part, to reform this thinking by bringing people face-to-face with the humanity of these precious children and, in the process, tearing down the walls of ignorance that consign them to second-class status—or worse.

Visitors to Phoenix immediately find their preconceptions challenged, if not overturned altogether. When they see these children laugh, cry, express hurt, frustration, love, just like everybody else—and detect their often sly sense of humour—they come away changed. Their perspective is broadened and deepened, giving them eyes to see through the disability to the child, to the dignity due them as fellow-travelers on the road of life.

I have mentioned that the children were scared, even ashamed and shy when we first brought them to Phoenix. Very few of them would talk or lift their eyes from the ground, so our first job as team was to help them feel secure, to feel safe, to feel at home, to feel loved. Within just a few days—like desert flowers after a spring rain—they started coming out of their shells, began interacting with the staff, and with one another, and it was not long before they all became friends.

In fact, something even deeper than friends.

English is not my first language, but even if it were, I don't think I'd be able to express my feelings as my eyes swept the room that day, and fell upon Alexandru whose story you may remember—isolated for so long in a corner of his house, perhaps propped against a bench in the yard, seeing other children running, jumping, playing and knowing that, somehow, for some reason, he was different.

Suddenly, here at the Centre, he and the others discovered other children like themselves. *Many* of them! Some with different challenges, some more able, some less, but *like* them! All at once they had entered a world where they came first! Where they're free to grow, and laugh and play and make a mess, and fail and, in the process, *learn*. Where they can help one another, share experiences, and, at least in some measure, regain lost childhood. Here were facilities designed to accommodate their needs. Here was a staff—a new family—that treated them with respect and love. Here were other children like them with whom to become friends.

Can you imagine what this felt like after a life of being locked away, surrounded by only two or three people whose interaction with you was often negative, who, perhaps not intentionally, treated you like a piece of human furniture whose constant needs were a burden?

I, for one, know very well how it feels. I've often been told that I'm different. My disability is the burden of dreams. Even friends and relatives would sometimes distance themselves from me, probably because many of them thought I had lost my mind. I don't blame them. I can't explain my transformation from someone who was, basically, clueless about the disabled, to one who's been called an obsessed crusader on their behalf.

That's okay. There are certainly worse things to be called.

Over the months and years, I've often thought—and I'm sure others did as well—'Who are you to change the stereotypes and attitude?' 'Who am I to take these children from their homes and show them a life, give them inclusion, and education?'

The Many Faces of Phoenix

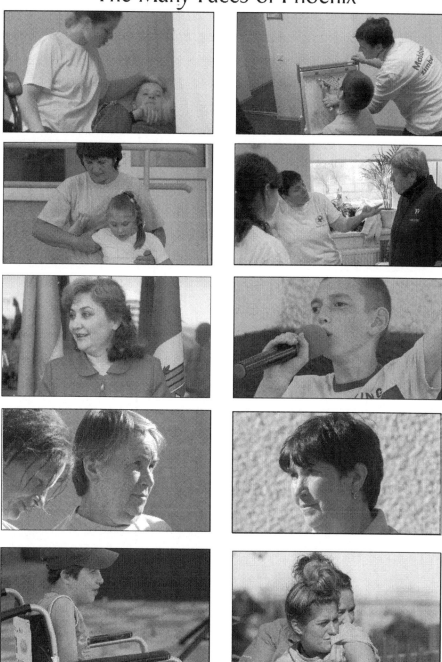

The question, for me, became 'Who would I be if I didn't?'

So a vision became an obsession, and obsession became a passion, and I think, in the end, only those with passion will bring about real and lasting change. John says I'm like a train without brakes. I guess that's as good an analogy as any. When it came to making Phoenix a reality for those children, I wasn't going to be stopped by the barriers of government obstructionism, traditional stereotyping, or general Moldovan pessimism. They would simply have to yield. There were no two ways about it.

Now, every day, children walk, stumble, crawl, or are pushed in wheelchairs through the doors of my dream; the place that so many said could never happen, is there. I can give you directions to it. I can point it out on Google Earth! Most importantly, I can show you the difference Phoenix has made in the lives of its children.

Some of the pioneer cast, crew, and friends at Phoenix

As I write, Phoenix had helped hundreds of children in its two departments. The Day Centre provides education, inclusion, transport, outings and cooked meals for 37 children. Some of them have already been able to enter mainstream education. There are around twenty children daily at Phoenix.

The Early Intervention and Rehabilitation centre provides treatment, physiotherapy and physiological help for very young children with special needs, or with restricted abilities. During its first year, we helped 120 children; all of them visited more than 2-3 times, for a few weeks at a time. Thanks to early intervention, three children went into mainstream education, and two were able to become day centre beneficiaries. Helping them early in their lives also helps their parents to give them better support with their physical problems.

Ask any one of these children what Phoenix represents for them, and the predominant answer will be: 'It's our second home'. Days off and holidays are like punishment for them. The first Christmas at Phoenix, one of our donors asked the children to write down what they wanted from Father Christmas. Bear in mind the age of children at Phoenix range between six and twenty, so we expected all sorts of answers. But everyone who was older than twelve said that their only wish was that Phoenix would never close, and we would not to stop them coming to it.

Most of the time, when I go back to Phoenix, it's to resolve an issue or address a problem and, because I have to get back to work—meaning fund-raising and schmoozing—I don't always have time to spend with the kids, and that's my heart's desire. Every time, when I leave, I'm left with their words ringing in my ears: 'Please, won't you stay with us?' That's what they really want, just my time. So I make a mental note that next time this will be the priority. It's always next time. So far, other than the days when I manage to take them out for a pizza or on an outing, that particular 'next time' hasn't come.

I can't explain to them that, though I'm often far away, I'm always there, and that they are always here, in my heart.

I want to close this chapter with one child's story, recorded by one of the Phoenix team. The theme is a common one within these walls:

'Natalia lives with her father and younger brother. From the time she entered Phoenix Centre, it became her home. This girl, whose disability is a lack of motor skills, had lived all her life in two rooms in her father's house. She had no personal experience of the greater world, of which she was only aware by what she saw on TV.

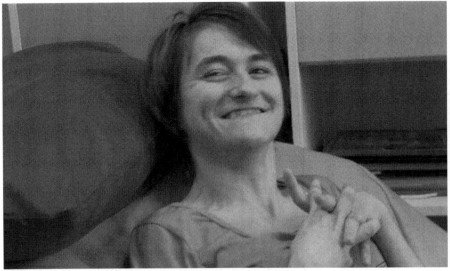

Natalia, always smiling goodwill ambassador of Phoenix Centre

Natalia has difficulty speaking and only on rare occasions would anyone have the patience to listen, or figure out what she was trying to say. When she came to the Phoenix

Centre, we saw a helpless child who could not maneuver in a wheelchair. She could not separate her hands or her feet and only could look at you with wide eyes and a helpless smile. She would say that the years she spent at home alone had been so difficult because she only saw a future without hope. Every day of every week was the same with the only joy being when her brother would come from school to talk with her. She was face to face with her fate as a child with special needs. At one point she began to hate life and sunny days.

The Phoenix Centre has changed Natalia's life. Here, at her second home, she always expresses how she has found joy in her soul and a dream of living and doing new things. She's learned to play checkers, make puzzles, color and draw, and create beautiful works of art. She has learned to eat fruit, cookies, and candies by herself, and drink without a straw. She has improved her motor skills enough to put away toys and objects and even manipulate her wheelchair and stand with assistance. Here she has found friends who have become family. Now her greatest sadness is the holiday when she has to stay at home. Her greatest desire is that the Phoenix Centre does not close.'

And, if I have anything to say about it, that will never happen.

Being possessed by a vision is a scary thing, but if you step through the fear, overcome the obstacles, and witness the achievement of your goals—in my case the smiles, the joy, the life brought to the children at Phoenix—it doesn't really matter if you are understood, or how many obstacle you had to overcome along the way, the feeling, when you are doing what you were put on earth to do and life makes sense, is like nothing else.

Chapter Thirteen
Phase II

To have a vision, then to make it real is just the first part of the battle. The second part is to keep it going. In regard to Phoenix Centre, this means not simply to maintain its viability, but to keep it fruitful, to make sure it continues to Make A Difference.

I know people often consider me rushed, unprepared, or just leading with my heart instead of my head. That observation is not entirely unfounded. However, from day one, I was hardheaded and practical enough to know that unless I could build something sustainable, it was not going to last. I knew I needed something to make money, a social enterprise. Accordingly, from those early days, I planned for the whole enterprise, including Phoenix, to become self-supporting. What I didn't realize at the time was that it would be impractical—well, let's say impossible—to do everything at the same time.

That had been my idea, initially: to build it all at once, and open all phases of the facility at the same time. In retrospect, I'm glad that didn't happen. With the benefit of hindsight I can see that attempting to do so would probably have killed me.

Just as there's a point at which the dream must bend reality to its will, there's also a point where the dream—for its own survival—must yield to reality. For me, that point was reached during the construction process, the management and oversight of which proved to be all the challenge I could handle. Had I attempted to take on more, it is the children who would have suffered. Phoenix would have been derailed by competing demands upon our time and resources. Instead, we had to use that time to come up with some sort of social enterprise as a step toward self-sufficiency.

As I've demonstrated, disabled children in Moldova and many ex-Soviet Union countries are isolated, even abandoned in many cases. But the dissolution of the Soviet Union, and the ebbing tide of emigration that Moldova has experienced since the 1990s, has put another huge weight on the country's severely strained resources: the elderly. Those who fought for the country, who had their minds set under communism and underwent the upheaval of intellectual and political revolution, whose livelihood was stripped from them after the dissolution, and who raised their families hand-to-mouth through poverty, drought, and ever-changing political hierarchies—our parents and grandparents—have been left alone.

It is a common refrain among this population that, for want of opportunity in their homeland, their children left the country as soon as they were out of school, establishing new homes, new families in their new host country. The refrain becomes a lament when they attempt to call to mind the last time their children visited them. Was it last winter? Last year? Year-before-last? When did I last see my grandchildren? What have they been told about me?

There was a time, not so long ago, when such questions would have been considered absurd; Moldova was a country where there *were* no care homes or nursing homes. They weren't needed. Families always looked after their own elderly. In fact, the security of senior citizens was in their children, and the confidence that they would care for them in their old age. 'I have 2-3 children. They will see I'm taken care of, just as I took care of them'.

Those children are gone.

For those who remain in Moldova, the question now is, who will provide for the care of these Senior Orphans—as I call them—as they advance into old age and are plagued by its inevitable infirmities? As we have seen, just as the state is not disposed to care for disabled children, neither is it equipped to care for its elderly.

This was made painfully evident in a visit I paid to a state nursing home. There are not many things I regret having done in my life, but that is one of them. I wish I had never done it. I really do. I will never be able to shake the image that experience imprinted on my brain, on my heart. What I saw were people whose only recreation was to stare at walls. Whose only purpose was to take up space and to breathe. Whose only hope was an end to life.

Let me take you there.

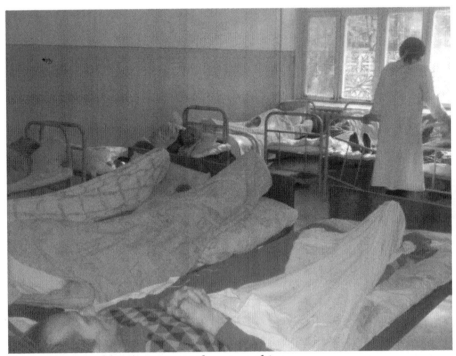

To be alive and living are not the same thing

The bedrooms are small—from eight to twelve feet wide, eighteen feet long. Three iron beds line each wall. On these are stained mattresses and sheets; on those are human beings, for whom this is home. Six people, sometimes more.

Some sick, some senile, some perfectly healthy in mind and body, but slowly succumbing to the burden of remaining alive in such surroundings, crammed into this space, hour-after-hour, day-after-day, year-in-and-year-out, with no prospect that things will one day get better.

The floors, walls, and windows are scrubbed and clean, but the air is redolent with the odor of bodies untended. In the middle of the narrow aisle that separates the rows of beds is a metal bucket. This, apart from the single lavatory they share with those in all the other similar rooms off the main corridor, constitutes the room's only concession to hygiene.

Worse still, I came upon an eighteen-year-old boy with no legs who, because of his disability, had been deposited here. There was no place else for him. Mentally, he was perfectly normal. I'd go so far as to say bright. Sharp. With who knows what potential? But here he lay; here he would stay. Here he would live a meaningless life and, when he ultimately died, cease to be a burden on the State—his greatest achievement.

I have never visited a Moldovan prison, but I doubt it's any worse than this. I left after ten minutes.

The comparison between the care home in the U.K. where I did ad hoc work together with my regular hospital work, was dizzying. In fact, there is no comparison. Each resident in the U.K. home had an en-suite bedroom and bathroom, in which outside visitors were made welcome. Residents can make trips to the country, the seaside, the theater, or the high street. They have a choice of items from a constantly varying menu, and many forms of entertainment. The main difference was unavoidable: they were living their lives. In Moldova, they were living slow death.

I had to do something about it. Why should an elderly person be forced to live by rules and timetables just because they can't look after themselves in their own home? Why can they not be treated with respect and dignity and given as much freedom as they want, to wake up at whatever time they want, and have their meals when it suits them. Why shouldn't they have a choice of appealing, nutritious meals, not standard institutional gruel? Why shouldn't they have whatever equipment they need to be mobile? Why not the transportation to take them where they want to go: to market, to church, and maybe to a concert—something amazingly few will ever have had the time or resources to do?

Three things: money, knowledge, and training.

I became determined to create a template at Phoenix Centre to show how elder care should be done, how it can be done, in Moldova. That's how I came up with the idea for Phoenix II, a residential nursing home as a private social enterprise. The first task was to formulate a scheme by which it would be self-sustaining, even profitable. I thought of my own case, with my mother living in Moldova and I in England. What would I do to prevent her from falling into the abyss of a State home? Would I be willing to pay for her care? Of course I would!

I recall like yesterday the day I took my mother to a restaurant for her birthday when she was visiting me in the U.K. For me, having a birthday at home, with a home-cooked meal is so much more enjoyable, but I didn't have time to organize that, so we thought we would take her out and invite my friends. She had tears in her eyes. When we were back home, she said to me that it was the first time she had been to a restaurant for herself, other than going to weddings. This statement numbed me. I hadn't realized how out of touch I was.

This brought to mind the hundreds and thousands of my brothers and sisters in the Moldovan Diaspora. Would they, too, be willing to pay for quality care for their parents and grandparents? I have no doubt they would, especially when they learn of the availability of an affordable facility with all the amenities of those in the U.K. Who would want less?

It is our hope and expectation that proceeds from the senior residence in excess of those required for its operation, will go to support Phoenix I, making the first two phases of the Phoenix Centre self-sustaining. So, in my view, I can kill a tree-full of birds with one stone: disabled children will have the education, medical attention, therapy, and inclusion they deserve; Moldovan expats will be able to provide their parents with exceptional care in a socially stimulating environment—where children and seniors can interact for mutual enrichment—and we will have created a working model for similar self-sustaining facilities that can be copied and replicated across the country.

As of this writing, the plans and drawings for Phoenix II are done, all to the highest European standards. The reaction to these plans, from many quarters— architects, planners, and government officials—was 'Why do seniors need en-suite bathrooms? Why one person to a room? Why a social lounge on every floor?' It's just crazy sometimes, how people go out of their way to find a negative where there is none. I won't tell you what I wanted to say, because children may be reading this, but my response was simply, 'If, heaven forbid, you should find yourself alone in the world and unable to care for yourself what kind of care would you want? That provided by the typical Moldovan model, or the European one?'

Phoenix II will be completed by 2018 and, like Phoenix I, will be a modern model for the country. As I write, we are raising money for it as well as to keep Phoenix running smoothly until such time as the Phoenix II can support it. Once completed, the facility will provide the best elder care in the country, and stand as a goal toward which others can strive.

It's an economic reality, that if Moldova is to survive—

to thrive—it will need investment. Investment that will carry projects such as Phoenix Centre from conception through completion, and provide a reasonable return to investors. Those investors must be able to have confidence in those initiating, managing, and sustaining the project to do so effectively, in a timely and professional manner. They must also be able to trust the Moldovan government to work in the best interests of the project, the investors, and the market they seek to serve, and to remove impediments to the success of these projects. The names of those impediments are bureaucracy and corruption.

With the establishment of Phoenix Centre, we have proven these impediments can be overcome, but the process was exhausting, and the battle continues, with the Hydra presenting new heads every other day. So I sharpen my sword. This monster is going to die!

As I write, we need £70,000 to complete Phoenix II, and I'm excited to see the miracles unfold that will provide it!

Early stage plans for Senior Centre. Actual rooms will be singles

Chapter Fourteen

Four Prime Ministers and a Queen

Have you ever felt inferior, due to some sort of prejudice or stereotype, or felt that someone is so much more powerful than you simply because of his job, class, or maybe even nationality? Growing up in Moldova and having a Soviet mentality, you address everyone as Mr. or Mrs., except for relations, for whom there are an assortment of names or titles. Basically, you could only call by their first name people of your age or younger.

This was how you spoke to people around you. In the case of speaking to a doctor, a mayor, government minister, or anyone else of elevated social standing, there was an even more noticeable difference. Many people, like those among whom I grew up, feel so inferior they would never dream of meeting someone like that.

While I didn't experience those times personally, I did inherit the mindset, at least to some degree.

When I came to the U.K. in 2004 I addressed everyone—my supervisors as well as those picking strawberries with me—as I would have in Moldova, and they would laugh. They kept asking me to call them by their first name. This felt very strange, but slowly, without my noticing it at a conscious level, my mindset was shifting. I was beginning to realize that all people, because of our shared humanity, are equal—each unique and perhaps gifted in their own way—but equal.

As I started getting used to calling people by their first names, I began talking to them all the same and, very soon, began to think of them all the same. After analyzing my months in the U.K., I became emboldened to speak to anyone—with respect, of course, but not with fear and trembling.

These days, the pendulum of my mindset has swung the other way. Now it annoys me when it seems one person, or group of people, are looking down on another. As I mentioned before, I had this experience many times during the construction work at Phoenix. When I held my first staff meeting at the Centre, I asked to be called by my first name. I thought this would make all seem more part of a team and eliminate the 'us' and 'them' mentality that often creates barriers between leaders and subordinates. I also intended that, by not singling out any particular individual for special treatment, we would all come to regard each other as equally important players on the team. This would not only validate each person's input and initiative, but make them personally accountable for the success of their area of responsibility.

Unfortunately, it has not happened overnight and the 'boss' mentality still persists. I'm often called Mrs. Dunford, even though I insist on being called Victoria. I am assured this is simply out of respect—and I certainly have no quarrel with respect that is offered freely, rather than organizationally enforced—but I also suspect it stems from having been embedded in the psyche of inferiority that the Soviet system inculcated in the Moldovan DNA when they ruled over us. It is that defect that both keeps one from rising above our situation, whatever it may be, and provides him or her a convenient excuse for not doing so. It's deeply rooted and will only be changed with time and patience.

Had my time in the U.K. not taught me this lesson, there's no way I could have brought myself to the attention of the powers-that-be in Moldova, much less addressed them as equals and challenged them with their responsibility to care for those unable to care for themselves.

When I first launched MAD-Aid, I didn't personally know any members of the Moldovan Embassy in the U.K., but

I thought it was important for them to be present at the opening. Bear in mind that all I had was an idea, a vision solely on paper. All we had was a bank account with a zero balance. However, this did not stop me from inviting the diplomatic mission. In exactly the same way, I thought we should invite our member of Parliament for the Isle of Wight. I didn't expect him to come, but his assistant called me and confirmed that he would. This was extremely encouraging, as was the fact that the Embassy staff came all the way to the island to participate, as well.

What I want to say here, and emphasize, is that *unless you ask, you never know*. What these officials did was to be present, and that gave me the courage, the drive, the push, to carry on with my plan. For them to offer their time to our newly established organization was very much appreciated. I also contacted the British ambassador in Moldova when I took the first load of aid, but unfortunately he was at the end of his mission and quite busy.

Later, when I took the 200 wheelchairs to Moldova, and called the newly appointed ambassador, Mr. Batson, he kindly agreed to join us for the event in Bălți where we distributed them. I was told, some time later, that I'd been pretty blunt with my invitation. 'Mr. Ambassador, are you coming or not?' That didn't leave him much room for refusal!

Now great friends, he and I often recall that episode with humor. It was not my aim to be rude. I think I was just so determined to have them there—to get them behind the project—that I was, shall we say, less than diplomatic.

I could approach these people, because I simply refused to be intimidated by them. Their worst response to my request could only be 'no'. But it might be 'yes'. Unless I asked, I'd never know. To make visions and dreams a reality, you just keep going, and the most important thing is not to limit your mind. Research individuals or organizations whom you intend to approach for help. Learn about them as best you can. A number of online sites like LinkedIn can be valuable resources in this regard; then write, e-mail, call and, if possible, visit them in person. That's what I was able to do, thanks to my change of mindset. If there was anybody out there who could possibly help me help those kids—with time, money, advice, equipment, donations, expertise or anything else—they were going to hear from me. And they were going to hear good and loud!

I'm never short of words when comes to talking about MAD-Aid. I know it inside out; why it started, when it started, and where it's going. I have my passion, my heart and my soul in this work, and the notes of my presentations are written on my heart. People see that.

The most important advice I have for anyone starting a project—anything from a charity or business, to a municipal program—don't even start if you don't have the passion to see it through. If you decide that you do, know your plans, purpose, and the processes by which they will be achieved, inside out, not just the elevator speech. If you do this, you never need fear being caught off guard by a question to which you don't have an answer. You never know who you could meet and when you could meet them and how they could influence you, or help you achieve your goals.

So here's a review of those I met along my MAD-Aid journey, and how I met them.

As a result of working with the Embassies, I found out about another organization in Moldova, the BRD (Bureau for Relations with the Diaspora), that was acting alongside the state chancellor under the Prime Minister. It forms a bridge between migrants who have left the country and the government agency in their county of origin. As soon as I found out about them, I thought they might be able to help by advising us as to who could fund the transport of those 3000 beds. Unfortunately, it was not possible so we lost the beds.

But that association led to an introduction to Mr. Leanca, the Prime Minister of Moldova at the time. I don't do politics, in any way or form—it's just not me—but he promised to support us and my work in Moldova in any way that he could. Sadly, this was not to be because only few months later his government collapsed. It is very hard when these things happen in Moldova (I assume it's the same in every other country) because all the ministers are changed and, in an atmosphere of uncertainty, projects like Phoenix fall through the cracks. As this was my first experience with government officials, I had put lots of hope into collaboration and working together with them to start making a difference in people's lives.

I wasn't prepared to surrender my vision to the political situation. As I worked to refurbish the daycare centre, I would need government advice, such as our VAT exemption status, and various licenses, among other things.

I met the new Prime Minister, Gaburici, at an embassy reception. He was young, energetic, eager to bring positive change to the country, and promised all the British charities his full support. Shortly thereafter, I made an appointment to meet with his chancellor, and things began to take shape. However, within a hundred days of taking office, Gaburici was out.

Welcome to Moldova.

After this, I decided not to waste time and energy courting the government anymore. There was no point. You can imagine, of course, how much support at that level—having those in power on the same page with you—would mean, but it just didn't seem to work in Moldova.

I gave up on the government and turned my attention to the work at the Centre, and getting ready for the opening.

A few weeks before the opening I was informed that the new Prime Minister, Strelet, had accepted our standing invitation to join the Minister of Social Protection, Mircea Buga, (an extremely good one by this time) and to come to the opening of the centre. The British Ambassador suggested to him that he should come, and BRD invited him officially, with my consent of course. He was impressed by the work we had done and officially said that he would meet me for coffee to talk about how the government might help.

And by now you can probably guess what happened next. The Strelet government collapsed too, less than a month after the opening of the Centre. Unbelievable, I thought! John joked that I had put all of them out of a job and maybe he should take me to meet the British P.M., whom he really didn't like. Of course, that was a joke, but I had met personally three Prime Ministers, and they hadn't lasted long enough for the milk to go bad. For Phoenix, and for Moldova, this was not funny. Between governments, the country stagnated even more, and the ministers of Health and Social Protection, with whom we worked closely, were replaced in a never-ending game of musical chairs, with each change of the executive locks.

As I write this—though not necessarily as you read it—the country has its forth Prime Minister since MAD-Aid started in 2012. I was in the same room with him at the Diaspora congress, but refused to be introduced to him personally because I figured he'd be gone by dessert.

As well as an assortment of Prime Ministers, I had the honor to have met many people who believed and trusted me, trusted my work and my vision, and joined me along the way.

I expect most of those who have struggled to breathe life into a vision can say this: everyone I've met on the MAD-Aid journey has taught me a good lesson—some good, some bad—but all were lessons I needed to learn and experience I can carry forward as Phoenix grows.

As for the hard lessons, I confess I'm still quite bad at identifying people with false motives. I'm a trusting person at heart and, working in a charity, I have a hard time believing that people would try to take advantage of me—or especially of the kids at Phoenix—but my trust has been abused more often than I care to admit. Some people *do* try to take advantage, and some even succeed.

That said, there are many, many people who, true to their word, have stood by me shoulder-to-shoulder through it all, and without them there wouldn't be a MAD-Aid or a Phoenix Centre or those medals. More importantly, the hundreds of children who have been and are being served at Phoenix would still be stuck away on their shelves, with the world passing by. The people who have shown themselves worthy of every confidence are the trustees, and our supporters and volunteers. These, I know, will be there if needed with no agenda other than to be helpful and to contribute towards making a difference.

Here's a random example: Recently Francisca de Zwager, who worked as a consultant for large companies, building them from the ground-up, volunteered to become my personal mentor. She spends hours and days showing me the right path and working with me with an eye toward making MAD-Aid even better and broadening its positive impact on the lives of people in need. Every day I wonder what I've done to deserve her and the many, many other wonderful people who go out of their way to help me, and Phoenix. For every person who shunned me because they believed I was getting rich from the charity, I was lucky to have ten others—often complete strangers—who understood and shared my vision and, over time, have become great friends.

I think every day how lucky I am.

I have found supporters from many parts of the world. For example, when I was running around MADly to open the

Centre, the Moldovan Ambassador to Canada, Ala Beleavschi, contacted me about an American couple, David and Barbara Crossman, missionaries who had moved to Moldova to help with charity projects. The Ambassador thought I was the best person to put them in touch with. Great, I thought. We have plenty of projects they can help with!

John and I met with David and Barbara briefly in Chisinău, where they live, on our way from Rîşcani back to the U.K. During that visit, I encouraged them to go to Phoenix, which they did a short time later. Afterward, they thought of many different ways to help. David created a lovely documentary and raised money for the daycare, and they are both always introducing more supporters and potential supporters to the Centre. We have since become great friends

With Barbara and David Crossman and Mariana

and they're sort of the honorary grandparents of the Phoenix family now. The children recognize them as soon as they come through the door.

These are just a couple of examples, though, of the many with which I could fill several books! I've met so many wonderful people, who feel the same as I, that we can make a difference. Some offer time, others advice; some offer their manpower, their skill, and know-how, and some provide funding. Everyone's help is needed and appreciated, and it's all of us working together that have made one woman's vision a reality.

I hope, for you and your dreams, this will serve as encouragement to keep an open mind, to never stop looking for answers, to never be afraid to approach someone—whoever they are, however lofty the position they may hold—and to ask for help. Someone will always come your way with just what you need to get you closer to your goal—sometimes just an inch, sometimes a mile, but always closer to the realization of your dream.

One of the side benefits, you might say, of MAD-Aid and its work, aside from introducing John and me to a host of wonderful people, is a number of awards I have been honored to receive on behalf of the entire team.

In December 2015, I received a phone call from the Moldovan President's office, inviting me to go the next day to be presented with a 'Civic Medal' for all the work we have done in the country. Yes, I was in the U.K., and yes, the invitation was for the next day. Of course, I couldn't go, but I was scheduled to fly over a few days later on charity work, so I was informed that they were having celebrations during the whole week, and my invitation was changed to another day. I was not sure what to expect. A medal of course, but why, and what would it look like, and how many kinds of distinction does Moldova have? I don't get too excited about awards, personally, but inasmuch as this kind of recognition publicizes Phoenix and validates the work of the people working there, they're important.

I made it to the ceremony, and it was quite a nice one. I shook the hand of the President of Moldova but, as I did, couldn't help wondering if he'd still be around by the time the flashbulbs cooled. There's no shortage of medals given in Moldova, and a lot were handed out at this particular ceremony. Truth be told, I'm not at all sure the President knew who I was, or why he was giving me a medal. Still, as far as I was concerned, it was an achievement for the entire team: the trustees, funders, volunteers, the U.K. and Moldova teams. And, miracle of miracles, the president lasted till his mandate ended! Maybe my jinx works exclusively on Prime Ministers!

Medals were certainly not a consideration when I envisioned MAD-Aid. Not once did I think that I would have a medal at some point. But it turned out there was more to come. In November 2016, John and I were Skyping, he on the Isle of Wight and I in Moldova.

'You got an official government letter in the post today', he said.

I told him to open it.

'I can't. It's got your name on it.'

'You don't have to read it, if you don't want to,' I said. 'Just hold it up to the computer and I'll read it.' All I could think was, had I run afoul of the U.K. government, despite all my efforts to make sure I was doing everything legally? Why else would I get an official letter?

When I read the letter, I was speechless. One of the first things it said was that it was strictly confidential, and I should keep it that way until New Year's Eve. I had been nominated for a British Empire Medal for my work to change the lives of children with special needs in Moldova! I could share this unexpectedly shocking good news with absolutely no one. Not for another six weeks.

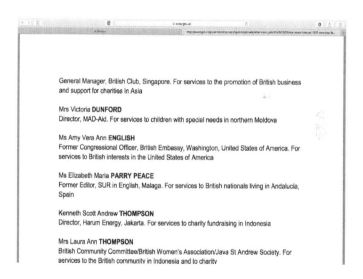

General Manager, British Club, Singapore. For services to the promotion of British business and support for charities in Asia

Mrs Victoria **DUNFORD**
Director, MAD-Aid. For services to children with special needs in northern Moldova

Ms Amy Vera Ann **ENGLISH**
Former Congressional Officer, British Embassy, Washington, United States of America. For services to British interests in the United States of America

Ms Elizabeth Maria **PARRY PEACE**
Former Editor, SUR in English, Malaga. For services to British nationals living in Andalucia, Spain

Kenneth Scott Andrew **THOMPSON**
Director, Harum Energy, Jakarta. For services to charity fundraising in Indonesia

Mrs Laura Ann **THOMPSON**
British Community Committee/British Women's Association/Java St Andrew Society. For services to the British community in Indonesia and to charity

Hey ho, I thought, it is only a nomination so I may not even be mentioned in the Queen's New Year's Honours List. In England, unlike in Moldova, honours are awarded twice a year, on New Year's Eve and on the Queen's official birthday.

And then I saw how proud my husband was. He wouldn't admit it, but he said, 'Our work is starting to get noticed'.

New Year's Eve came and the list appeared, and indeed I was there!

My first email went to our trustees, and the person I thought had nominated me. And then I called my mother. Of course, she does not need for me to have medals in order to be proud, but I knew she was the main reason I got it. By the next morning I'd put the news on Facebook, thinking that it was important for supporters, volunteers, and staff alike, to understand that it was everyone's medal, not just mine.

What I didn't realize was that this would make quite big news in Moldova. One headline read: 'First Moldovan to get a medal from the British Queen'. Again, this was not a plan. I never worked towards a distinction or medals; I work to change lives, to bring purpose to children's lives and smiles to their faces. *They* are the ones who are really important. But I was extremely honoured and grateful that the charity was noticed and all the hard work—and the transparency with which it had been accomplished—had paid off. I also suspected it would mean that more people would join us on this journey.

And I was right.

The BEM came with an invitation to attend the Queen's Royal Garden Party at Buckingham Palace. All the protocol was fascinating. I was allowed to bring one guest with me. Of course, I wanted John. This was going to be one of the very important days in our life. Originally John suggested auctioning his place and raise funds for MAD-Aid, but in the end, we didn't have much time before having to declare the name of the guest, and I really wanted him there. Very few people understand that MAD-Aid has been possible only because of him and his support from the shadows, where he always prefers to remain.

The Buckingham Palace experience was other-worldly, and something that even most British-born people don't have the chance to see. John summed it up: 'We got sandwiches with no crusts and Royal tea, and a medal for take-away.'

If my goal had been to get to the Palace, I might never have gotten there. But that was never my aim or desire. I take it as a reward for us all for the extremely hard climb over rocky roads to get where we are today. Remember that I started the charity to transform one hospital ward, and together already, we had managed to do so much more.

What a wonderful journey it has been!

MAD-Aid had come a long way.

I've come a long way.

The lesson for those of you with dreams is this: If it's possible for a fatherless girl from a tiny village in northern Moldova, to trek from the deeply-rutted and muddy roads of her youth to Buckingham Palace gardens and tea with the Queen, then *anything* is possible!

You never know where the road might lead!

It was a long trek, and a difficult one, but if I had the chance to change anything in my life, I wouldn't. These experiences, the good and the challenging, are what have made me who I am today. Every dream will meet opposition. Count on it. Expect it. Plan for it. But don't yield to it. My advice is this: understand that muscles only grow in opposition. The same is true of character, resilience, and determination. When you encounter opposition, then, remind yourself, your future won't be determined by the opposition you face, but by your response to it.

Was I disappointed at times? Of course. Discouraged? After all I've told you in these pages, it would be odd if I said, 'No, of course not.' Many times frustration pushed me almost to the breaking point. But through it all I acquired the skills that enable me to talk to anyone, fearlessly and boldly. I learned how to network and make connections between people. I became a strong believer in the view that we can do almost anything when we pull together, but that that initial tug has to come from within each of us, and it begins with a desire to serve, and to make the world a better place for others. No change for the better is too small. No effort, no sacrifice is too insignificant even if all it does is bring laughter to a child's eyes. There are multi-billionaires who have never achieved that much.

In the end, each of us is responsible for his own life and, as far as I'm concerned, life is best lived that reaches out to help others. In this, we all have a part to play, no matter how abundant or meager our gifts. This is our duty as citizens of the world. It is our privilege as members of the human race.

How would I sum it all up?

First, don't stop at the first door. If it's locked, open another one, and if it's not possible to find the right door, build one from scratch. Think who you know that might be able to help, or to open that door for you. People won't know you need help or support until you let them know. So ask! You may get a hundred 'Nos,' but sometimes all it takes it one 'Yes'.

J.K Rowling met with one refusal after another when she presented her manuscript for Harry Potter to publishers. But she refused to give up, not because she wanted to become a billionaire, but because she believed in her story. She was passionate about it, and she was ready to get up every time she got knocked down.

Does hard work always, inevitably, lead to success? No. But I know one thing: success won't come without it. Life proves over and over that dreams are much more likely to become reality for those willing to work for them, who learn the art of letting go of what is not important to focus on what is.

Secondly, if you make your way up, don't say, 'Why should I help others? No-one helped me to get where I am!' That's an attitude I often hear from Moldovans when I try to explain why they should get involved. And it's not true. No successful person got where they are without help from anyone. If they think that, they're deluding themselves. Life is for all, and it is to be shared. That's the only way we can hope to make the world better place.

'Change begins with every single one of us'
(V. Dunford personal quote)

Chapter Fifteen

'You Can *Do It!*'

'It always seems impossible until it's done.'
Attributed to Nelson Mandela

I would like to ask you to start this chapter with an open mind and a simple question: 'What are the three things you want to accomplish in life?' For some of you, this will be easy. You're first reaction will be 'Only three!?' Others will struggle to come up with three things for their Bucket List.

And then there is always the child whose only wish is for a world with no stairs...

Now look at your list. I'll tell you something about it: The first and most important step in ticking them off is *believing* they're possible, and that *you* can do them. The next step, is preparing yourself to ignore those who tell you it can't be done—and there's no shortage of them! There were many days when I was depressed, upset, and frustrated. At those times, I felt so lonely and vulnerable in the face of a mountain of problems that I couldn't resolve, and couldn't afford to hire someone to solve them for me. The secret is that pretty much no one knew how scared and worried I was. I knew that if people didn't have confidence in me, I wasn't going to get them to back me, so I always put on a brave face and looked for solutions.

It's also important that your list not be cast in stone. As we grow, as we experience life, our horizons expand, our perspective changes, and so do our interests and passions. Go back to your list every now and then and amend it accordingly.

In the nineties, for example, there would have been only two items on my list: survive and study. That makes for a very small world, one in which the thought of visiting other countries had no place. The possibility of travel never crossed my mind. All I had to do was what lay before me each morning, help mother run the home, go to school, and study. But even these basic things, I did with all my heart. I finished at the top of my class.

Scratch one item off my mental bucket list. Now add a new one: continue my formal education. To what end? As I thought about it, a distant dream—long submerged in my subconscious—reared its head: I wanted to be a doctor; another item on the list.

Then I considered the reality of what that would entail. Medical school would take nine years and cost a fortune. I knew that my mother and brother certainly couldn't afford it, and it wouldn't be fair to expect my mother to help me for that long. In Moldova, student loans do not exist, so I'd have to get a job to help pay the bills. But full-time study meant five full days a week at university, and study over the weekend, leaving no time for a job on the side. Reluctantly, I decided pursuit of a medical degree would be selfish.

Strike an item off my list. (It's a good idea to write your list in pencil!)

I then considered Business and Economics as a second choice, but that would mean a course of private instruction, for which I would have had to pay on contract. Another non-starter, but that one hadn't even made it on the list.

Finally, I decided to study chemistry, which was closer to medicine and which I thought would be affordable. I passed the admission test at first go, and even got a bursary that paid for the entire five years. From the third year, I started working night shifts selling flowers in a 24/7 flower boutique. I was becoming pretty self-sufficient. But still, my aspiration during those years was to study English and computer, and learn to drive, none of which were cheap. Did I give up? Of course not! I knew one day I would be able to do them.

Well, almost. The computer courses are still on the list, but in the meantime I learn what I need from webinars and YouTube videos. As for driving, I've studied and passed my driving license twice: once in Moldova and once in the U.K. When it comes to mastering English, I guess you could say I'm engaged in a program of life-long learning, which may sound odd, given that I've written this book. But there's no better way to learn than by doing, and I get a little better at it every day.

You begin by knowing what you really want, and deciding you're going to do whatever it takes to get it done. Remove the words 'I can't' from your mental vocabulary, and replace them with 'I will.'

Let me give you an example.

By the time I was twenty-five years of age, with my still extremely broken English, I opened my first business in the U.K., a shop selling Eastern European foods. Did I have any business knowledge? No, and probably not even much business sense, looking back, but I still did it. I learned, I made mistakes, learned from the mistakes, and moved ahead. This was when I learned one of the most important lessons: don't fear failure. Thomas Edison experimented over a thousand times before he found the right filament for his light bulb. If he'd given up after one less experiment, the world might still be in darkness.

There may be many stops and starts along your journey, but the only real failure is stepping off the train before it takes you where you want to go!

Are you guaranteed success? Of course not. Life is full of too many variables, and you have to accept that and be prepared to accept the consequences. At a seminar once, I was talking with a girl from the United States, and discussing the famous film, *The Secret*, which postulated that anyone could become a millionaire. She said that wasn't true, to which I replied, 'The film is right, and so are you. The opportunity exists for anyone to become a millionaire, but does everyone want to be a millionaire? It's a question of priorities.'

Some people only want a full-time, secure job, and a regular paycheck, and that's fine; that's their aspiration and if that makes them happy, it is pointless to attempt to entice them to the risk of starting a new business, or attempting something outside their comfort zone. But we need millionaires as well, because it is they who invest in the ideas and innovations that form the basis for new businesses, that, in turn, provide new jobs and pay the wages of people for whom security is most important.

Of course, working hard is not always equal with working smart.

The question you have to ask yourself is, do you believe enough in your dream to sacrifice everything to it, even your fear of failure? Are you willing to do all you can to bend the odds in your favor? I found a book by Susan Jeffers called *Feel the Fear and Do It Anyway* that helped me get a handle on this issue.

You can only do what you want, and can receive back only what effort you put in.

Family members and friends often tell me, 'What you've done is good, but it doesn't bring you money. With your abilities, you should run your own business, and be rich!' There's some truth in that, but the work we do in MAD-Aid has given me riches far beyond material wealth. Will I concentrate on business one day? Maybe. But one thing I will never do is put money before humanity.

Look at your bucket list.

Given what you've learned from my story, which of those things is so important to you that you'd be willing to make whatever sacrifices are necessary to bring them to pass? If any of the items doesn't meet that standard, strike it out. Of the one(s) that remain—to which your answer to this question is a resounding, not timid, 'Yes!' —your next step is to start gathering information and making the contacts necessary to lay the groundwork upon which to build your dream.

Life is unpredictable. It is out of our control in many cases, but we need to take the responsibility to change what we can. We often tend to have aspirations or demands that we don't really want or need, just because of the influence of our surroundings. For instance, your neighbor has a house with a swimming pool. Does that mean you should want one, too? What about the celebrities you see in magazines or on the telly living in castles, surrounded by servants, driving expensive cars, yachts, and planes? Is that what you want?

It takes a certain amount of maturity to stop and ask yourself two important questions: First, *Why* do you want those things? That's an existential question that only you can answer. Assuming you answer that question to your own satisfaction, you next have to ask yourself whether you're willing to invest your time and resources in a house with a pool, or a castle, car, yacht, or plane, and assume responsibility for them. (A wise man once said, *'We are possessed by our possessions.'*). If so, fine. But begin with realistic expectations of the work it's going to take to get— and keep—those things.

If you discover that your dream—perhaps one you have carried forward from youth—is not really in line with the goals you have today, have the courage to let it go. Only then can a new one take shape in its place.

Life is too short for *ifs* and *buts*. Analyzing the past too much really does not move you forward. Get out there and embrace the challenge! I can assure you 100% that it's going to be extremely hard and difficult—it will even seem impossible at times—but keep your focus on the destination.

I can relate this attitude to my feeling about flying: I absolutely love it. But I hate the travel experience; living on the Isle of Wight makes even the simplest trips complex. However, this will never stop me from traveling and the desire to discover new places, new worlds, new cultures. I am focusing on the destination. If the journey is difficult, even unpleasant, so be it. In fact, perhaps anticipating the difficulties of the journey, and preparing for them, can even help us enjoy them!

I'll work on that.

'If you can dream it, you can do it.'

If you have it in your mind to start something—an organization, a business, a project of any kind—try to surround yourself with positive people who will support your idea, even if they can't necessarily help. The kind of people who will let you fly and ease you back to earth when you fly too high. Think of it this way: which would you rather have for companions on your long-awaited holiday, negative people, or positive people?

Apply the same criteria to the journey toward your dreams.

With MAD-Aid I was very lucky that, despite having so many people who did not agree and thought my idea was bad, I had, more importantly, positive people, like John, who is always extremely supportive, and my trustees, who, God bless them, have found a way to manage me and keep my feet on the ground without pouring cold water on my plans.

It's never too late to start doing what you love, never too late to start living, loving, trusting. Open the cage! Embrace freedom! Do I like driving? Not really. But I really

160

love the freedom it gives me, the freedom to choose when and where I want to go.

England, for me, was the equivalent of a mental, emotional driver's license. It opened my mind to whole new worlds of possibilities, without and within. It changed my perspective, and with it, my attitude, and these have given me the opportunity to see the world with new eyes. So have the many books I've read over the years.

My biggest enemy was in my own mind, my own negative inner voice. It's taken all my strength and determination, and the education I've acquired through experience, to overcome it. Once I did, I became free to put a name to my dream: Phoenix, and to do what I had to do to put flesh on its bones and bring it to life.

Chapter Sixteen

Success Starts with 'No!'
How do you start a project?

I've learned that almost anything can be done, and is most often done best, by those willing, even eager, to work together. Changing the world is a common goal of leaders, politicians, missionaries, those in the medical field, scientists, researchers. No plan, however great or well founded, will succeed without every single one of us, because we all have different gifts and abilities, and it is only by bringing those ingredients, if you will, together that the chances of success are optimized.

The same is true of starting an organization; it's only possible if you build a team. The primary task of a visionary— apart from having the vision in the first place—is to define it for others, and convey your enthusiasm for it with such confidence that people are drawn to it. Next, identify the strengths and weaknesses of those people, and delegate responsibilities to those best equipped to handle them successfully. Much of that success will depend your ability to inspire cooperation.

In many ways, starting and running a charity organization is like building a family from scratch, and families have to learn to live together. You may not like a sibling or some other relative, but you're stuck with them, so make the most of it! At the root of it, they're probably the gravity that keeps your little planet from flying off into outer space. In a charity organization—or any other organization— it's a good idea to remind yourself that you might have a lot to learn from those who rub you the wrong way. It takes friction to sharpen a blade. If you work together and really make an effort to see the best in those around you, which, unfortunately seems to fly in the face of human nature, you'll go so much further, much faster.

However, this requires the time and skill to understand who you can trust and who you can't. I have a tendency to place trust in people too easily, I think, because I attribute to everyone the same standards I live by. This has led to some painful lessons.

I have also learned that, while people may make promises with the best of intentions, I mustn't take actions based upon those promises until, as the saying goes, 'the check has cleared the bank.' This applies not only to money, of course, but to pledges and promises of materiel, manpower, and assistance of many kinds. If you expect to be disappointed sometimes, you're less likely to let those times discourage you and knock you off track.

In the last five years, John and I have traveled over 100,000 miles between us on charity work. Many of those miles have been spent traveling to meetings that turned out to be a waste of time and money, and some ended in pleasant surprise when our expectations were exceeded. Either way, we travel mostly to make a difference and to see what others are doing to make a difference. In the process, I made the mistake of trying to make time for everyone. With tending the home, working full-time, volunteering at a care home, fund-raising, running an organization that required at least five employees, and being answerable to my board of directors, time management, which is critical, became impossible.

It's then I realized that time is my most precious treasure, and it's limited. You have no idea how much of it is left. If you lose your possessions, you can always replace them. If you lose your health you can, often with hard work and good medical care, get it back. But time is a commodity that once gone is gone forever.

Getting older you get to understand that not everyone deserves your attention, but it is really hard to choose who does. Running a charity takes many skills that I am still trying to develop. One of the most important among these is the courage and heart to say 'No' to so many sad cases that need help, need your organization, need you. Yet, you can't help, not because you don't want to, but because it is impossible to do everything.

When the news about my British Empire Medal hit the Moldovan press, together with thousands of messages of congratulation, I received desperate pleas from people for whom we were the last hope.

Here's a small sample of the messages I received and the response when I had to say 'No':

'Please help me to work in the U.K. in a hospital'. When I explained that this was not in my power, the answer was really brutal: 'You're just like the government; you do one small thing and then just capitalize on it to get publicity'.

Here's another. 'Please allow my child to go to your centre.' I had to explain that, since the girl lives 250 kilometers away, and the centre is not residential that would not be possible, the reply was, 'Well then, why do you say that you help disabled children?'

The list goes on. How do you deal with that? If the answer exists, I am still looking for it.

It made me stop and think, 'What am I doing wrong? What more can I do? How can I divide myself into more of me?' On days like this, sometimes weeks, all I wanted to do was disappear, to just work in quiet and be left alone. But when I'd take a break, the people who were accustomed to my full-time attention felt ignored, and would get upset. I'm reminded that even Jesus had to go away into the desert from time to time, just to get away from the demands everyone was making on Him and to regain His strength. It's hard to explain that sometimes.

Neither John nor I have had much quiet time since MAD-Aid started. That's not good, and it's something we need to pursue with intention for the health of our relationship, as well as for our own physical and mental well-being. Without those, how can we be of use to anyone else?

I've been asked numerous times over the years, 'Why do you do this?' Sometimes the question is asked by someone who is suspicious of my motives, sometimes simply out of curiosity. My answer is always the same: I didn't start MAD-Aid because I had too much spare time on my hands, and nothing else to do. I didn't start it because I had plenty of surplus money, or was brimming with experience and knowledge. I didn't do it for medals, or recognition of any kind. I simply saw people in need and wanted to help. It's that simple. And if, in the process, I was able to bring something back to the country where I was born, where my heart is, so much the better.

The Phoenix Team - pulling together!

Once thing I've never said—and you will have gathered by reading this far—is that it's been easy. But difficult doesn't mean impossible. If a dream doesn't motivate you to step outside your comfort zone, you're unlikely to have the fire in the belly it will take to jump the hurdles standing between your dream and its realization. On the other hand, if you and your dream have hold of one another and both simply refuse to let go—and you regard 'impossible!' as a great starting point—then go and do it. To start a charity, a business, or any similar enterprise *is achievable* only if you accept that people and circumstances will constantly rise to oppose you, and you resolve, before hand, to refuse to let them stand in your way.

I had all the motivation I needed to form this resolve when I thought of the children our charity would serve. I'd looked into their faces and, for me and for John, there was no turning back.

Here's an example of one child at our centre—a girl named Alexa, who is seven years old. This is from her case report (name changed for privacy):

Alexa then:

Alexa lives with her mother and father. She came to us at the Phoenix Centre with infantile cerebral paralysis. Alexa could only say 'Papa', 'Mama', and the word for water 'apa'. Beyond that she would make certain sounds and scream until she was tired and go to sleep. She could not walk without her mother's support. She could not feed herself, or even hold a spoon in her hand. She was clumsy and wore diapers. She would scream and lose patience with herself while playing games with other children. She was unable to stay in one place for an extended period of time, and often refused to take part in activities, but could not be left alone.

Alexa now:

Alexa has changed enormously. The most gratifying fact is that she recognizes the children in the group and attempts to call them each by name. Though she does not clearly speak each name, she is still understandable. With Alexa we work with the images on cards and she communicates very well; her vocabulary is increasing by leaps and bounds. At Phoenix, she has learned to feed herself, to keep the spoon in her right hand, take it to her mouth and eat slowly and neatly. Now she can walk alone and only in rare cases, requires help. With that support, she can even walk up and down stairs! She also plays with the other kids, and enjoys herself immensely. Several of the older children watch over her. She still finds dressing, undressing and going to the toilet herself very challenging, but she's determined to master them. And she will.

Alexa's mother cannot believe the changes she sees in her daughter.

Alexa's story is not unique; we have hundreds of stories like this, and they help keep me in focus and concentrate my energies on what can be changed, and what I can do, rather than keep getting upset and sad about things I cannot do and people I can't help.

I'm often reminded of the famous serenity prayer by theologian Reinhold Niebuhr (yes, I looked that up!):

> *God, grant me the serenity*
> *to accept the things I cannot change,*
> *Courage to change the things I can,*
> *And wisdom to know the difference.*

Part of my vision is that every person in Moldova who needs a wheelchair should have one, and to have some sort of Red Cross centre in each district with spare wheelchairs in it. It still seems like a dream and much is needed in order to do achieve it, but I aim to work even harder because experience has taught me that it's possible and that I can do it.

Speaking of experience, I've learned so much over the years, mostly by trial-and-error, so allow me to offer a list of things I would do if I had to do it all again.

1. Define your mission clearly: Who do you want to serve, and why?
   NOTE: **Please** *bear in mind that, as much as you might want to, it is impossible to help everyone.*
2. Decide on your geographical area of work.
3. Build a strong board of trustees and advisers
4. NOTE: *Don't just get friends on board who are likely to rubber stamp anything you propose for fear of offending you. The best, most practical ideas and practices often evolve from opposition, from their consideration from a variety of perspectives and experience. I was extremely lucky that I had a number of highly educated, honest neighbours who formed my non-executive board. They have held my feet to the fire, and I'm so grateful for them.*
5. Write your constitution for your charity and be clear of your aims and your procedures for running it.
   NOTE: *This document is your road map. Frequent reference to it will help keep you on course when diversions and detours arise, which they will almost daily.*
6. Register with the appropriate government body. For example in the U.K., with the Charity Commission; in Moldova, with the Minister of Justice.
7. Plan the strategy for your first year.
   NOTE: *This is a snapshot of the steps you will take during the first year toward fulfillment of the goals in your constitution.*

It's important that this document be flexible enough to accommodate changes beyond your control, but firm enough to stand on when the storms arise.

8. Brand your enterprise carefully, with a logo, colors and slogans that are short and memorable, but that will also explain your work in your chosen field.

   NOTE: *Don't short-change branding as superficial or secondary. Multi-national corporations spend billions of dollars on branding for a very simple reason: it works. Name recognition is critical to their survival. The importance of image holds no less true for start-ups. A good, attractive and cohesive branding package—logo, business cards, stationary, website, brochures, and so on—conveys the notion that the same thought, care and effort have gone into branding will carry on throughout the project. While this can't be expected to engender trust in you among perfect strangers, it will earn you a second look and, if all goes well, the right to prove yourself.*

9. Find as many partners as you possible can. Collaboration is the key.

   NOTE: *It's been said that the one-armed sailor can only row in circles. Consider yourself that one-armed sailor. There are many oars on the little ship in which you're about to embark on a journey on stormy seas, and each needs to be manned by a strong sailor.*

10. Open a bank account and make sure you

have two signatures on it. Most banks will require that, but just in case they don't, doing so protects you and the charity.

11. Go and shake the world until it yields to your dream.

Below are the skills you'll require immediately. This doesn't mean you have to possess all of them—though the more you know about them, the better—but it will help you look for and recognize those abilities in others, so you'll know who to ask for help.

1. Charity Management
2. Project Management
3. Writing and reporting Grants
4. Fundraising
5. Event organizing
6. Managing Volunteers
7. Logistics
8. Social Media and communications.

Keep in mind, you're going to make mistakes; sometimes big ones. We all do; it's part of our claim as human beings—and that's what we are ahead of any distinction we acquire as ditch-diggers, scientists, doctors, teachers, preachers, researchers, lorry drivers, rocket scientists, able or disabled—human beings. As such, our highest calling is to help others achieve the most that it is in their capacity to achieve.

That's what I hope this book, in some measure, has done for you. Now, go and live your dream, and know that the most worthy dream of all, is that which makes someone else's dream come true!

Epilogue

Just Life

A Day in My Life

Whether I'm in my house on the Isle of Wight, at the Phoenix Centre in Rîşcani, or my mother's house in the village of Mihaileni, my day begins with the ringing of the radio alarm. A new day begins. Yesterday's *To Do* list doesn't matter. Often, because events over which I had no control threw all my plans out the window, many of the items on that list just get transferred to today's *To Do* list.

When I'm in the U.K., my days are somewhat predictable. Once I drag myself out of bed and get breakfast, I do probably the worst thing I can – I sit down at the computer. Once I slip into that zone – answering and writing e-mails, Skyping with the staff at Phoenix, writing grants, scheduling events, updating my board – John has to almost physically pull me out of that chair and away from that screen for a walk down to the seafront for some fresh air. Otherwise the day slips by and, before I know it, it's 18.00 and I've been staring at the screen for nine or ten hours – or more. So, I try to force myself to go out during my lunch hour for that walk, come rain, sun, or wind.

Still, it doesn't happen as often as it should.

In Moldova, my first may last for as long as 48 hours: I pack my suitcase, take the suitcase to the car, drive the car to the ferry, take the ferry to the mainland, drive to the train, take the train to the airport, fly to Chisinău – Welcome to Moldova! – pick up a car, and drive to Phoenix Centre.

It may have been only been a few weeks since I left, but necessity has called me back. I have two phones, and from the moment I land and switch them on, the Moldovan number, especially, is rarely quiet. I attempt to meet with everyone, because in the last few years, fate has brought many wonderful people to me, and I try not miss any opportunity. I'm traveling between Chisinău and Rîşcani pretty much every other day, sometimes with a driver, most of the time by myself.

At Phoenix Centre, I can hear the children as soon as I get out of the car, and if anyone is looking through the window, you can hear them shout: "Victoria is coming!" At the door, always, Vadim is first to greet me. He is an 18-year-old boy with Down's Syndrome who, though his comprehension is very good, did not speak for 17 years. Since coming to Phoenix, he's learned "mama', "da", which means "yes" in Romanian, and "hello". But to say he can't speak is not to say he can't talk. In excited grunts and illustrative gestures, he guides me to the classroom and, in his own way, tells me everything that is going on.

In the classroom, I first give the girls a cuddle. Natalia, with her uncoordinated hands, does not let me go until she can give me a proper hug. I say "hello" to my colleagues, and I'm just about to leave the room and go upstairs to salute the rest. But a look at the boys stops me in my tracks. The look on their faces let's me know that they expect a cuddle as well. Fortunately, I have plenty of those to go 'round. That's the wonderful thing about love, the more you give, the more you have to give!

Arriving in the office, I find hundreds of issues that have accumulated since I last left, and I only have a few weeks. The aim is the same regardless of where I am: to raise funds for MAD-Aid and for the Phoenix centre, or to distribute the equipment that has been stored away since my last visit. Time is flying very fast and we need to arrange the next convoy of humanitarian aid. Logistics, planning, recruiting and coordinating with drivers, writing up wish lists and connecting with hospitals and other agencies who have items to donate and arranging for their collection, and a hundred-and-one other things; among them one request leaves me numb, a family desperate for clothes, shoes, and wood to see them through the coming winter. What do I have for them? How can I get it to them? Suddenly, all my plans take second place to this request. But it's only the first of six or seven similar ones.

So much for schedules.

At 18.00, everyone has gone. Phoenix is silent. Finally, I have time to answer a few emails. I expect there will be quite a few, because I've been traveling, so I open my laptop aiming to work for an hour or so. The next time I look at my watch, it is 21.00. I'm exhausted, but I realise I haven't been to see my mother yet, and I know very well that she is waiting for me, with dinner too, probably. I get up, feeling guilty, and drive to the village, where a nephew is waiting for me too, with a big smile, eager to open my suitcase. Tomorrow is another day.

Will it be longer or will I be smarter??

The days and weeks fly past in a whirlwind of activity, until finally it's time for me to go back to the U.K. I say "goodbye" to the children who have reproached me already many times: "Again you didn't have enough time to stay and talk to us". I make the same mental note: next time that's a priority. Next time.

And I'm back on the plane...

Life is an education. Learn from it!

10 lessons I've learned in my 35 years:

1. Change starts with every one of us

This is my motto and I think about it pretty much every day. If you don't like something it is very likely in your power to change it. If not, perhaps it's your attitude toward it that has to change.

2. Savour Life

We are a generation that is always running, literally and indirectly, without time, without stopping to appreciate the moment, especially the simplest and nicest moments. I love sunsets and sunrises, and my neighbour makes nice pictures of them from the place where I live. I often scold myself for not taking the time to just sit and enjoy the beauty of the world around me. Simple moments like this I believe need to be appreciated, as do the many people around you, those who seek the shadows as well as those who seek the spotlight.

3. Find a *Way*, Not an *Excuse*

You'll always find people who will tell you how much can go wrong, negative people who will tell you that what you want is impossible, or is too hard. Taking that kind of advice to heart is the coward's way out. By all mean, listen to advice – good, bad, or indifferent – but take responsibility for the final decision yourself.

4. You can't please everyone

Some people like me, some people are indifferent, and some dislike me, some may even hate me. If I spent my time trying to please everyone along that spectrum, I'd go mad. Well – even madder. When all is said and done, you have to live with yourself – and doing that with a clear conscience means being willing to look at yourself, to be honest about your sins and shortcomings, and work to correct them. Let others think what they will, I have more important things to do than worry about their negative thoughts of me, or what I'm doing.

5.   Everything is Possible!

Ever since I arrived in the U.K. in 2006, I have lived following this motto. I believe all of us have the same opportunities and pretty much the same channels to take from life all we want. The difference is that some are willing to work for their dreams and are determined to do whatever it takes to give them the best chance of success. Others wait for the dream to just materialize from thin air, as if the universe owes them something. Lastly, there are those who live for payday and spend the week marking time until the weekend, when life begins and ends. To which of these groups would you say 'Everything is Possible' applies?
In which group are you?

6.   The Future is not the past

Changes are inevitable. There is no point in following our predecessors by doing things exactly the same way as they used to. It is a new era, a new world and we need to adapt to it, especially in Moldova. It is important to start thinking multi-dimensionally, outside the box. It is important

175

in my view to create your own life, write own book following real principles and values, not the stereotypes and prejudices of society.

7.   Read and Grow!

As I mentioned earlier, advice in books has helped me solve many problems. But I don't just read those related to the work of MAD-Aid and Phoenix; I read to be inspired, to acquire knowledge and fresh, challenging perspectives, as well as to just enjoy a good story!

8.   Money is a Tool, Not a Measurement of Worth

Money is only an instrument, that's all. Why are people killing for money, or running after it all the time? All that really matters in this life cannot be bought: health, love, happiness, time. From the moment learn to do what you love, and love what you do, the value of money is directly related to its ability to help you do it.

9.   Mistakes: Your Best Friends in Disguise

An infant struggles to her feet, attempts her first step, and falls on her face. Wouldn't a loving parent scoop her up in their arms and forbid her to try walking again for fear she might get hurt? Of course not. Each time she tries, she'll correct a mistake she's learned from. In no time, she'll be running! Mistakes are common to every human endeavor, and the only way to avoid them is never do anything. Understanding this helps us to be more forgiving of others – and ourselves – and turns mistakes, and the people who make them, into blessings in our lives. A thick catalog of errors is something we, as human beings, all have in common. Some teach us what to do, some what not to do, but each will either teach us how to fly, how to land, or how get up and get on with it.

10.   Expect the unexpected.

When I was talking about doors opening when you least expect it, I have to remember that this can go either way. You will hear often, "live your every day as if it were your last, because one day it will be".

Here is a very personal example:
When we delivered hundreds of wheelchairs and saw how happy the people were, and we could see that they could go outside now, and we knew we were making a difference. I knew that the hospitals needed to be improved and beds changed and so much more.   However, I never fully understood how much this difference means in real terms, until March 2017, when I received a call from Moldova, and was told that my brother had fallen off a ladder and broken both ankles. I was the first person to be informed, before my mother, even before his wife. He had already been taken into hospital.
At moments like this I try to force myself to act first and panic later. Sadness can kick in when I've done everything in my power to help. I called his doctor first, got his x-rays emailed to me within an hour, spoke to a British orthopedic doctor with whom we'd worked on a few projects, made a plan and then called my brother. He is stronger than me, he always was. But even so, he said to me, "please take me from this hospital or I will crawl on my knees and go home". This was my brother, with two broken ankles in a hospital which John and I had managed to provide with a lot of new equipment. Unfortunately, none of it had made its way to the orthopedic ward, where my brother was.
However, with help from from friends we managed to

arrange his surgery in a private hospital. Also because of MAD-Aid he was able to have a wheelchair, an elevating bed, specialized transport, and a bedside commode within hours of the accident.

I took him out of the hospital the same day.

And then I took a step back and even as I write now, I can't comprehend what other people do, who don't have a relative to step in and advocate for them. He will probably have some sort of limp forever, but thanks to expensive surgery he will be able to put shoes on, and walk on both legs. But it has opened my eyes so much more. Expect the unexpected. Only when something happens to people around you, can you understand that helping when you can, and when it is needed, will never be forgotten. I now more fully understand what life is like for a person who can't go outside for long periods of time simply for want of a wheelchair.

I often get asked, "how many people has your organization helped?" It's a question I can't answer. For every child we help, who knows how many lives are positively impacted? Two? Three? A hundred? It's also a question I won't answer, because it reduces human beings to columns of numbers, which they were never designed to be. MAD-Aid doesn't help in order to count, it counts because it helps Make A Difference -
and so can *you*!

God bless *your* dreams!
With Love
Victoria

THE END

The Phoenix Gallery

The Phoenix Gallery

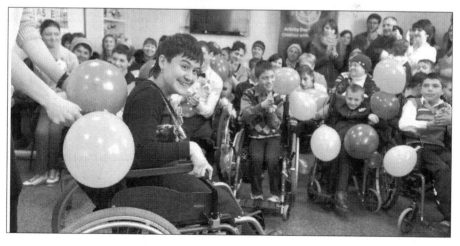

The Phoenix Gallery

The Phoenix Gallery

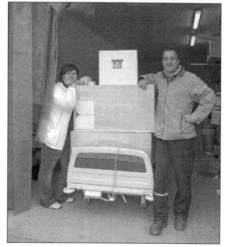

The Phoenix Gallery

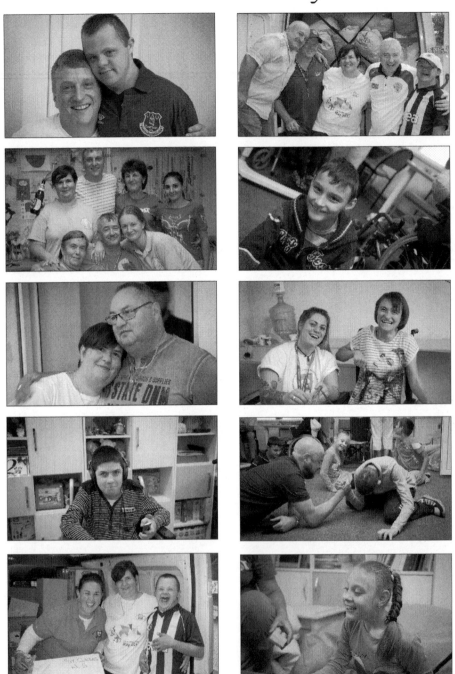

Images on this page from Brian Ryan Photography

The Phoenix Gallery

Our Trustees

Ann Barnes

Peter Lewis

Ann Lewis

Iurie Bivol

Our Moldovan staff - the heartbeat of Phoenix

MAD-Aid
Registered Charity 1150955
Company No: 8317917
Telephone: +44 1983 718408
Mobile: +44 7426594664
Email: info@mad-aid.org.uk
55 Cambridge Road
East Cowes,
Isle of Wight, PO326AH

www.mad-aid.org.uk

Printed in Great Britain
by Amazon